VEGETARIAN
COOKBOOK

For Cheese Lovers

VEGETARIAN
COOKBOOK

For Cheese Lovers

Tonya Buell

Cumberland House
Nashville, Tennessee

Copyright © 2003 by Tonya Buell

Published by
    Cumberland House Publishing
    431 Harding Industrial Drive
    Nashville, Tennessee 37211

Cover design: Unlikely Suburban Design
Text design: Mary Sanford

Library of Congress Cataloging-in-Publication Data
Buell, Tonya.
  Vegetarian cookbook for cheese lovers / Tonya Buell.
     p. cm.
  ISBN 1-58182-346-0 (pbk.)
  1. Cookery (Cheese) 2. Vegetarian cookery. I. Title.
  TX759.5.C48B84 2003
  641.6'73—dc21

*To my mother, who taught me how to cook
and is still teaching me.*

Contents

Introduction

I've never met a cheese I didn't like. Growing up, I was mostly exposed to a few "all-purpose" cheeses: mozzarella on pizza, Parmesan on pasta, blue cheese in salad dressing, and Cheddar for everything else. As I got older, I started experimenting with other types of cheeses, and I began to discover a whole world of cheeses that had previously been unknown to me: soft, creamy French cheeses; smoky Dutch cheeses; crumbly Mediterranean cheeses; and zesty, sharp cheeses. Ahhh . . . the ecstasy of it! I was hooked.

My favorite course invariably became the cheese course, rare in America but plentiful throughout Europe. And, here in America, where I can't very often get an entire plate of cheese, I often insist on a meal with at least some cheese in it.

Being a vegetarian, I have begun to realize more and more the benefits that cheese can provide—aside from its wonderful and varied taste. The elusive complete protein, so difficult for vegetarians to come by unless one wants to eat tofu every day, is abundant in cheese. Furthermore, as a woman I am well aware of the need for calcium in our everyday diet, and, wouldn't you know it, cheese comes through there too!

Yes, I realize that cheese can be fattening. My friends and family never seem to let me forget that. But what's a little fat compared to the fabulous benefits—number one of which is taste—that cheese provides? I know, I know, I can hear you now, telling me that fat is bad, bad, bad; but, in fact, we all need *some* fat in our diets. If you absolutely must, you may use low-fat cheeses for the recipes in this book. But don't, by all means, skip the cheese! Life is way too short.

So enjoy the recipes in this book. If you are a vegetarian, you probably already understand how difficult it can be to find delicious vegetarian recipes that satisfy your taste buds as well as your conscience. If you're not a vegetarian but are leaning in that direction, maybe this book will convince you to take the plunge! You too can eat delicious, protein-rich meals without eating those poor critters we all love so much. Try it!

VEGETARIAN
COOKBOOK

For Cheese Lovers

APPETIZERS
AND SNACKS

BLUE CHEESE BALLS

1   cup crumbled blue cheese
½   cup butter or margarine, melted
1   cup all-purpose flour
½   teaspoon seasoned salt
½   cup finely chopped almonds

Preheat the oven to 375°. In a small bowl beat the blue cheese and butter or margarine together with an electric mixer. Beat in the flour and seasoned salt until smooth. Place the almonds in a small bowl. Roll the blue cheese mixture into 1-inch balls, and roll in the almonds to coat. Place on an ungreased baking sheet, and bake for 12 minutes or until lightly browned.

MAKES 2 DOZEN

SPINACH BALLS

2   10-ounce packages frozen chopped spinach
2   cups herb stuffing mix
1   cup grated Parmesan cheese
4   eggs, beaten
¾   cup butter or margarine, melted
½   cup finely chopped onion
½   teaspoon garlic salt
¼   teaspoon pepper

Cook the spinach according to the package directions and drain. Allow to cool. In a large bowl combine the spinach with all of the other ingredients and mix well. Chill for at least 2 hours.

Preheat the oven to 350°. Roll the spinach mixture into small balls and place them on an ungreased baking sheet. Bake for 20 minutes. Serve warm.

MAKES 5 DOZEN

HOT SWISS CHEESE BALLS

3 cups grated Swiss cheese
2 tablespoons all-purpose flour
4 tablespoons sherry
Salt, pepper, and paprika to taste
6 egg whites, beaten
Crushed butter crackers
Vegetable oil

In a medium bowl mix together the Swiss cheese and flour. Add the sherry, salt, pepper, and paprika, mixing well. Fold in the egg whites. Form the mixture into 1-inch balls, and roll in the cracker crumbs. In a skillet heat the vegetable oil and fry the cheese balls until golden brown. Drain and cool before serving.

MAKES 5 DOZEN

BROCCOLI BITS WITH HONEY-MUSTARD SAUCE

1   egg
1   cup milk
½   cup all-purpose flour
½   teaspoon baking powder
½   teaspoon salt
½   teaspoon olive oil
2   cups broccoli florets, chopped
1   cup shredded Cheddar cheese
½   cup vegetable oil

Honey-Mustard Sauce:
3   tablespoons Dijon mustard
4   tablespoons honey

In a mixing bowl beat together the egg and milk with an electric mixer. Sift the flour, baking powder, and salt together into the egg mixture, and beat well. Beat in the olive oil. Stir in the broccoli and Cheddar cheese, and mix well. In a large skillet heat the vegetable oil over medium-high heat. Drop the broccoli mixture by spoonfuls into the oil, and fry until golden brown. Drain on paper towels and let cool.

To make the sauce, in a small bowl whisk together the mustard and honey.

MAKES 2 DOZEN

NUTTY GOAT CHEESE BITES

1	French baguette, cut into ½-inch slices
8	ounces spreadable goat cheese, softened
½	cup finely chopped pecans
12	seedless grapes, halved

Spread each bread slice with 1 tablespoon goat cheese. Sprinkle with pecans. Place half a grape, cut side down, in the center of each slice.

MAKES 2 DOZEN

DILLED CHEESE CUBES

1   loaf French bread
½   cup butter or margarine
4   cups shredded Cheddar cheese
2   teaspoons dill weed
1   teaspoon Worcestershire sauce
1   tablespoon diced onion
2   eggs, beaten

Remove the crust from the bread, and cut the bread into 1-inch cubes. In a medium saucepan melt the butter or margarine and Cheddar cheese over low heat. Stir in the dill weed, Worcestershire sauce, and onion. Transfer the mixture to a bowl, and beat in the eggs. Dip each bread cube into the cheese mixture, coating thoroughly. Place the cubes on an ungreased baking sheet, and chill for at least 4 hours.

Preheat the oven to 350°. Baked the chilled cubes for 10 minutes.

MAKES 5 DOZEN

BAKED CHEDDAR OLIVES

1   cup grated Cheddar cheese
2   tablespoons butter or margarine,
    softened
½   cup all-purpose flour
⅛   teaspoon cayenne pepper
1   3-ounce jar pimiento-stuffed green
    olives, drained

In a bowl combine the Cheddar cheese and butter or margarine.
Add the flour and cayenne pepper, and mix well. Mold 1 tablespoon of the mixture around each olive, covering it completely.
Place on an ungreased baking sheet, and chill for 2 hours or until
firm.

Preheat the oven to 400°. Bake for 15 minutes or until
golden. Serve warm.

MAKES 2 DOZEN

STUFFED CELERY

4 ounces whipped cream cheese

1 8-ounce can crushed pineapple, drained

2 bunches celery, rinsed and cut into 4-inch stalks

In a medium bowl mix together the cream cheese and pineapple. Spoon the mixture into the celery stalks. Chill for at least 1 hour before serving.

MAKES 3 DOZEN

STUFFED CUCUMBER SLICES

1 large cucumber
3 ounces cream cheese, softened
1 tablespoon crumbled blue cheese
1 teaspoon grated onion
2 teaspoons finely chopped fresh parsley
½ teaspoon dill weed
Sliced pimientos

Cut off one end of the cucumber, and scoop out the pulp. In a small bowl combine the cream cheese, blue cheese, onion, parsley, and dill weed. Spoon the mixture into the hollowed-out center of the cucumber. Wrap in plastic wrap and freeze for 2 hours.

Slice the chilled cucumber into ¼-inch slices, and garnish the slices with pimientos.

MAKES 1½ DOZEN

STUFFED JALAPEÑOS

12 fresh green jalapeño peppers
1   cup grated Cheddar cheese
3   ounces cream cheese, softened
½   teaspoon Italian seasoning
2   eggs
1   tablespoon milk
⅔   cup dry breadcrumbs
    Ranch-style salad dressing

Preheat the oven to 325°. Cut each jalapeño pepper in half lengthwise and remove the seeds and pulp. In a medium bowl beat together the Cheddar cheese, cream cheese, and Italian seasoning. Spoon the cheese mixture into each pepper half. In a small bowl beat the eggs and milk together. Place the breadcrumbs in another bowl. Dip each pepper half into the egg mixture, and roll in the breadcrumbs. Place the pepper halves, filled side up, on an ungreased baking sheet, and bake for 30 minutes. Serve with ranch dressing.

MAKES 2 DOZEN

STUFFED PARTY MUSHROOMS

16 ounces fresh whole mushrooms
¼ cup grated Parmesan cheese
¼ cup dry breadcrumbs
¼ cup finely chopped onion
½ teaspoon oregano
¼ teaspoon salt
⅛ teaspoon pepper
1 clove garlic, minced

Preheat the oven to 350°. Remove the stems from the mushrooms and set the caps aside. Finely chop the mushroom stems. In a medium bowl combine the chopped mushroom stems and all of the remaining ingredients; mix well. Place the mushroom caps on an ungreased baking sheet and fill with the cheese mixture. Bake for 20 minutes or until thoroughly heated. Serve warm.

MAKES 3 DOZEN

STUFFED SNOW PEAS

5   ounces snow peas
8   ounces soft spreadable herb cheese

Steam or blanch the snow peas for 20 to 30 seconds. Remove the string from one side and cut a pocket into each pea pod. Using a small spoon, fill the pods with herb cheese. Cover and chill for at least 1 hour before serving.

MAKES 4 DOZEN

CHEESE SPIRALS

16 ounces cream cheese, softened
1 package Ranch-style salad dressing
    mix
2 green onions, minced
4 12-inch flour tortillas
½ cup diced red bell pepper
½ cup diced celery
1 2-ounce can sliced black olives
½ cup shredded Cheddar cheese

In a medium bowl combine the cream cheese, salad dressing mix, and green onions. Beat with an electric mixer until fluffy. Spread one-fourth of the mixture on each tortilla. Sprinkle the bell pepper, celery, black olives, and Cheddar cheese over the cream cheese mixture. Roll up the tortillas, and wrap them tightly in aluminum foil. Chill for at least 2 hours.

Cut the rolls into 1-inch slices to serve.

MAKES 2 DOZEN

SPINACH PITA CRISPS

4   6-inch pita bread rounds
2   cloves garlic, cut in half
4   cups fresh spinach leaves
½   cup red bell pepper, sliced and
     roasted
3   tablespoons feta cheese, crumbled

Split the pita rounds in half crosswise to make two rounds. Toast under a conventional broiler or in a toaster. Rub each toasted pita half with garlic and set aside. In a 1½-quart casserole dish place the spinach and microwave on high until the leaves begin to wilt, about 1 to 2 minutes. Top the pita halves evenly with the spinach, red pepper strips, and feta cheese. Microwave on high until the cheese begins to melt, about 2 minutes. Cut each round into 6 wedges and serve warm.

MAKES 4 DOZEN

CALIFORNIA RAREBIT

3 tablespoons butter or margarine, softened

½ cup dry white wine

2½ cups grated Monterey Jack cheese

1 egg, beaten

1 tablespoon Worcestershire sauce

½ teaspoon basil

2 cups sliced fresh mushrooms

½ teaspoon garlic powder

12 slices white or sourdough toast, quartered into triangles

In the top of a double boiler melt 1 tablespoon of the butter or margarine. Add the wine and slowly stir in the Monterey Jack cheese until melted. Stir in the egg, and cook, stirring constantly, for 1 minute. Add the Worcestershire sauce and basil. In a separate pan heat the remaining butter and sauté the mushrooms until just tender. Sprinkle the mushrooms with the garlic powder. Arrange the toast triangles on individual heatproof plates. Spoon the cheese sauce over the toast and top with the sautéed mushrooms. Broil until bubbly.

MAKES 6 SERVINGS

CUCUMBER SANDWICHES

12 ounces whipped cream cheese
1 package Italian-style salad dressing mix
24 slices cocktail rye bread
2 cucumbers, peeled and thinly sliced

In a small bowl mix together the cream cheese and salad dressing mix. Spread the cheese mixture on the rye bread, and top with cucumber slices.

MAKES 2 DOZEN

GARDEN VEGGIE SQUARES

1 8-ounce package refrigerated crescent rolls

8 ounces cream cheese, softened

½ package Ranch-style salad dressing mix

½ cup chopped red bell pepper

½ cup chopped green bell pepper

½ cup chopped fresh mushrooms

½ cup chopped onion

Preheat the oven to 375°. Roll out the crescent rolls onto a large baking sheet to form a large, flat rectangular shape. Bake for 11 to 13 minutes or until golden brown. Allow to cool.

In a medium bowl beat together the cream cheese and salad dressing mix. Spread the cheese mixture over the cooled crust. Sprinkle with the red and green bell pepper, mushrooms, and onion. Chill for approximately 1 hour. Cut into bite-size squares to serve.

MAKES 4 DOZEN

PIZZA PUFFS

1	7-ounce package refrigerated biscuit dough
1	teaspoon oregano
1	cup grated mozzarella cheese
2	tablespoons pizza sauce

Preheat the oven to 375°. Cut the biscuit dough in half crosswise to form 2 rounds per biscuit and place the halves side by side on a large baking sheet. Using a spoon make an indentation on top of each biscuit half, and sprinkle oregano and mozzarella cheese into the indentations. Top with pizza sauce. Bake for 10 minutes or until golden brown and bubbly.

MAKES 2 DOZEN

PARMESAN RYE FINGERS

½ cup butter or margarine, softened
15 slices rye bread, crusts removed
1 cup shredded Parmesan cheese

Spread the butter or margarine over each slice of bread. Sprinkle with the Parmesan cheese. Cut each slice into 4 strips, and broil for 2 minutes or until the cheese is completely melted.

MAKES 5 DOZEN

CALICO CHEESE FINGERS

¼ cup shredded Monterey Jack cheese
¼ cup grated Parmesan cheese
½ cup mayonnaise
¼ cup finely chopped onion
2 tablespoons finely chopped fresh parsley
8 slices white or sourdough bread, crusts removed

In a small bowl combine the Monterey Jack cheese, Parmesan cheese, mayonnaise, onion, and parsley, and mix well. In a broiler, toast one side of the bread slices. Flip and spread the cheese mixture on the untoasted side. Broil until bubbly. Cut each slice into 3 strips to serve.

MAKES 2 DOZEN

SWISS ON SOURDOUGH

2 cups grated Swiss cheese
½ cup sour cream
2 tablespoons minced green onion
1 tablespoon lemon juice
½ teaspoon Worcestershire sauce
¼ teaspoon salt
1 8-ounce can water chestnuts, drained
3 6-inch sourdough rolls

Preheat the oven to 400°. In a small bowl combine the Swiss cheese, sour cream, green onion, lemon juice, Worcestershire sauce, and salt, and mix well. Slice 10 water chestnuts into thirds and set aside. Finely chop the remaining water chestnuts and add to the cheese mixture. Slice each sourdough roll into 10 slices. Spoon about 2 teaspoons of the cheese mixture onto each slice. Top each with 1 water chestnut slice. Place on an ungreased baking sheet, and bake for 12 minutes or until bubbly.

MAKES 2½ DOZEN

FRUIT CHEESE KABOBS

2 cups fresh strawberries, rinsed and halved

8 ounces grapes, rinsed

1 15-ounce can chunk pineapple, drained

1 cup cubed sharp Cheddar cheese

1 cup cubed Edam cheese

1 cup cubed Muenster cheese

Toothpicks or cocktail skewers

Thread the fruit and cheese onto toothpicks or cocktail skewers. Serve immediately or cover, refrigerate, and serve within 6 hours.

MAKES 2 DOZEN

ONION CHEESE SKEWERS

⅓ cup olive oil

¼ cup balsamic vinegar

Salt and pepper to taste

1½ pounds pearl onions, blanched and peeled

12 ounces Fontina cheese, cut into ⅓-inch cubes

Toothpicks or cocktail skewers

Preheat the oven to 375°. In a medium bowl whisk together the olive oil, vinegar, salt, and pepper. Place the onions in a roasting pan and add the oil and vinegar mixture; toss to coat. Bake for 25 minutes, or until tender. Remove the onions from the oven and let cool. Thread the onions and cheese cubes on toothpicks or cocktail skewers. Serve at room temperature.

MAKES 2 DOZEN

CHEESE BISCOTTI

½   cup butter or margarine, melted
1   tablespoon sugar
2   eggs
1   cup shredded sharp Cheddar cheese
2¼ cups all-purpose flour
1½ teaspoons baking powder
½   teaspoon salt
¼   teaspoon ground red pepper

Preheat the oven to 325°. Lightly grease a large baking sheet. In a large bowl beat the butter or margarine, sugar, eggs, and Cheddar cheese with an electric mixer until well blended. Gradually beat in 1 cup of the flour, the baking powder, salt, and red pepper. Beat in enough of the remaining flour until a soft dough forms. With a wooden spoon stir in more flour until a stiff dough forms. Divide the dough in half. Shape each half into a log and place on the prepared baking sheet. Bake for 30 minutes or until golden brown. Remove the logs from the oven and cut diagonally into ½-inch thick slices.

Reduce the oven temperature to 300°. Place the slices on the baking sheet and bake for 15 to 20 minutes or until the slices are dried but not browned, turning once. Allow to cool before serving.

MAKES 3 DOZEN

CHILI-CHEESE PUFFS

1¾ cups all-purpose flour
½ teaspoon seasoned salt
½ teaspoon garlic salt
½ cup butter or margarine, melted
½ cup sour cream
1   cup shredded sharp Cheddar cheese
¼ cup diced green chiles

In a medium bowl combine the flour, seasoned salt, and garlic salt. Cut in the butter or margarine until the mixture is crumbly. Stir in the sour cream, Cheddar cheese, and chiles, and mix well. Cover and refrigerate for at least 4 hours.

Preheat the oven to 375°. On a lightly floured surface roll out the dough to ¼-inch thickness. Cut into 1- to 2-inch circles with cookie cutters, and place on an ungreased baking sheet. Bake for 15 minutes or until golden.

MAKES 5 DOZEN

BLUE CHEESE CRACKERS

¼ cup butter or margarine, melted
1 cup crumbled blue cheese
1 cup all-purpose flour
2 tablespoons finely chopped almonds
⅛ teaspoon pepper
2 tablespoons milk

Preheat the oven to 350°. In a large bowl combine the butter or margarine and blue cheese, and beat with an electric mixer until well blended. In a small bowl stir together the flour, almonds, and pepper. Add the flour mixture to the cheese mixture and beat well. Gradually stir in the milk to form a thick dough. Divide the dough into two equal portions for rolling. On a floured surface, roll to about ⅛-inch thick. Cut into 1½-inch circles and place on an ungreased cookie sheet, making sure the edges do not touch. Prick each cracker 1 or 2 times with a fork or knife. Bake for 15 minutes, then flip each cracker with a spatula and bake for an additional 5 to 10 minutes, or until medium brown. Cool before serving.

MAKES 5 DOZEN

CHEDDAR CRACKERS

1½ cups all-purpose flour, sifted
1 teaspoon baking powder
½ teaspoon salt
  Dash cayenne pepper
½ cup butter or margarine, melted
2 cups finely grated extra sharp
  Cheddar cheese

In a mixing bowl combine the flour, baking powder, salt, and cayenne pepper. Slowly cut in the butter or margarine. Blend in the Cheddar cheese with a fork or wire whisk until well blended. Shape into 2-inch rolls and chill for 45 minutes.

Preheat the oven to 400°. Slice each roll into slices about ¼-inch thick. Bake on an ungreased cookie sheet for 10 minutes. Remove from the cookie sheet and allow to cool before serving.

MAKES 6 DOZEN

CARAWAY CHEESE CRISPS

3 cups grated Cheddar cheese
1½ cups all-purpose flour
½ cup butter or margarine, melted
½ teaspoon caraway seeds
¼ teaspoon salt

Preheat the oven to 450°. In a large bowl mix together the Cheddar cheese, flour, butter or margarine, caraway seeds, and salt. Place the mixture on wax paper, and knead by hand until all of the ingredients are well blended. Shape the dough into ½-inch balls. On an ungreased baking sheet, place three dough balls in a cluster, and flatten to ¼-inch thick. Repeat with the remaining dough balls, placing the clusters about 2 inches apart. Bake for 10 to 12 minutes or until lightly browned. Remove from the oven and allow to cool before serving.

MAKES 5 DOZEN

GARLIC PARMESAN CRISPS

½ cup butter or margarine, melted
2 teaspoons garlic salt
4 6-inch pita bread rounds
3 tablespoons grated Parmesan cheese
2 teaspoons basil

Preheat the oven to 325°. In a small bowl mix together the butter or margarine and garlic salt until well blended. Split each pita in half crosswise to make two rounds. Spread each round with the butter mixture. Sprinkle with Parmesan cheese and basil. Cut each round into 6 wedges and place on an ungreased baking sheet. Bake for 8 to 10 minutes or until crisp.

MAKES 4 DOZEN

SESAME CHEDDAR STICKS

1½ cups all-purpose flour
½   teaspoon salt
2   tablespoons sesame seeds
1   cup shredded Cheddar cheese
½   cup butter or margarine, melted
3   tablespoons Worcestershire sauce
2   tablespoons cold water

Preheat the oven to 450°. In a mixing bowl combine the flour, salt, and sesame seeds. Cut in the Cheddar cheese and butter or margarine. Sprinkle with the Worcestershire sauce and water. Stir together with a fork until well blended. Shape into balls and place on a lightly floured surface. Roll out the dough to ¼-inch thick. Cut into strips about 3 inches long and ½-inch wide. Place the strips on an ungreased baking sheet, and bake for 8 to 10 minutes or until golden. Remove from the oven and allow to cool before serving.

MAKES 3 DOZEN

CURRIED CHEESE TOAST ROUNDS

12   slices white bread
¼   cup chopped green onions
1   cup grated mild Cheddar cheese
1   2-ounce can chopped black olives,
     drained
¼   teaspoon curry powder
½   cup mayonnaise

Toast the bread and cut each slice into 2 rounds with a biscuit cutter. In a medium bowl combine the green onions, Cheddar cheese, olives, curry powder, and mayonnaise, and mix well. Spread the mixture onto the toast rounds. Place on an ungreased baking sheet, and broil until the topping begins to bubble. Serve immediately.

MAKES 2 DOZEN

BEER CHEESE FONDUE

2   cups shredded sharp Cheddar cheese
2   cups shredded Swiss cheese
2   tablespoons all-purpose flour
½   teaspoon dry mustard
¼   teaspoon pepper
1   clove garlic, halved
1   cup beer
    French bread, cubed

In a medium bowl combine the Cheddar cheese, Swiss cheese, flour, dry mustard, and pepper, and toss until well mixed. Rub the bottom and sides of a 2-quart saucepan with the garlic and add the beer. Cook over low heat until bubbles begin to form. Gradually add the cheese mixture, stirring, until the cheese is melted and the mixture is smooth. Serve with cubed French bread.

MAKES 4 CUPS

CHILI CON QUESO

1½ cups cubed American cheese
⅔ cup milk
¼ cup salsa
   Tortilla chips

In a saucepan combine the American cheese and milk over low heat, stirring, until well blended. Transfer to a serving bowl and stir in the salsa. Serve with tortilla chips.

MAKES 2 CUPS

RANCH-STYLE BEAN DIP

¼ cup butter or margarine
1 small onion, chopped
1 jalapeño pepper, seeded and finely
    chopped
1 clove garlic, minced
1 15-ounce can pinto beans, drained
1 cup shredded Monterey Jack cheese
    Corn or tortilla chips

In a medium saucepan melt the butter or margarine. Add the onion, jalapeño pepper, and garlic, and sauté for 5 minutes or until tender. Place the beans in a medium bowl, and mash with a fork. Stir into the onion mixture. Cook, stirring constantly, over low heat until hot but not boiling. Stir in the Monterey Jack cheese and cook until the cheese begins to melt. Serve with corn or tortilla chips.

MAKES 2 CUPS

SILKY APRICOT CHEESE DIP

¾ cup apricot preserves

8 ounces cream cheese, softened

1 cup sour cream

1 teaspoon almond extract

¼ cup blanched slivered almonds

In a small bowl combine the apricot preserves, cream cheese, sour cream, and almond extract. Beat with an electric mixer or whisk until very smooth. Fold in the almonds; cover and chill for at least 1 hour. Serve with crackers.

MAKES 2½ CUPS

RICOTTA FRUIT DIP

4 cups Ricotta cheese
2 tablespoons sugar
1½ teaspoons vanilla extract
1½ teaspoons grated orange peel
¾ teaspoon cinnamon
   Apple and pear slices

In a blender combine the Ricotta cheese, sugar, vanilla, orange peel, and cinnamon, and mix until very smooth. Pour into a bowl, cover, and chill for at least 1 hour. Serve with apple and pear slices for dipping.

MAKES 5 CUPS

ARTICHOKE CHEESE SPREAD

3   6-ounce jars quartered artichoke
    hearts, drained
1   small onion, finely chopped
1½ cups shredded mozzarella cheese
1   cup grated Parmesan cheese
1   cup mayonnaise
    Pepper to taste
    Italian-seasoned dry breadcrumbs
    French bread, toasted

Preheat the oven to 350°. In a bowl mash the artichoke hearts
with a fork. Add the onion, mozzarella cheese, Parmesan cheese,
mayonnaise, and pepper, and mix well. Place the mixture in a
shallow baking dish and sprinkle with breadcrumbs. Bake for 10
minutes or until bubbly. Serve with toasted French bread.

MAKES 4 CUPS

BLUE CHEESE SPREAD

1   cup crumbled blue cheese
4   ounces cream cheese, softened
½   cup finely chopped walnuts
½   tablespoon parsley flakes
    Bread or crackers

In a blender combine the blue cheese, cream cheese, and walnuts, and process until thoroughly mixed. Transfer to a serving bowl, and sprinkle with parsley flakes. Serve with bread or crackers.

MAKES 2 CUPS

FETA SPREAD

8 ounces cream cheese, softened
1 4-ounce package herb and garlic feta cheese, crumbled
1 tablespoon milk
⅛ teaspoon pepper
  Crackers or mini toasts

In a mixing bowl combine the cream cheese, feta cheese, milk, and pepper. Beat with an electric mixer until well blended. Cover and chill for at least 1 hour. Serve with crackers or mini toasts.

MAKES 3 CUPS

GORGONZOLA AND GOAT CHEESE SPREAD

1	tablespoon minced shallot
1	tablespoon snipped fresh chives
3	ounces Gorgonzola cheese
3	ounces cream cheese, softened
5	ounces goat cheese, softened
½	cup finely chopped walnuts, toasted
2	tablespoons finely chopped fresh parsley
	Crackers or toast

In a mixing bowl combine the shallot, chives, Gorgonzola cheese, cream cheese, and goat cheese. Beat with an electric mixer until smooth. Transfer to a serving bowl, and sprinkle with walnuts and parsley. Serve with crackers or toast.

MAKES 3 CUPS

OLIVE CHEESE SPREAD

8   ounces cream cheese, softened
¼   cup grated Parmesan cheese
1   tablespoon sliced pimiento-stuffed
     green olives
1   tablespoon sliced black olives
2   teaspoons chopped fresh chives
¼   teaspoon pepper
½   cup blanched slivered almonds
1   tablespoon chopped fresh basil
     Crackers

In a medium bowl combine the cream cheese, Parmesan cheese, green olives, black olives, chives, and pepper, and beat with an electric mixer until well blended. Cover and chill for 1 to 2 hours. Transfer to a serving dish, and sprinkle with almonds and basil. Serve with crackers.

MAKES 3 CUPS

PINEAPPLE-CHEESE SPREAD

2   cups grated sharp Cheddar cheese
1   8-ounce can crushed pineapple,
    drained
¼   cup finely chopped green bell pepper
2   tablespoons snipped fresh chives
1   teaspoon soy sauce
½   cup chopped pecans
¼   cup mayonnaise
    Crackers

In a medium bowl combine the Cheddar cheese, pineapple, bell pepper, chives, soy sauce, pecans, and mayonnaise, and mix well. Refrigerate 2 to 3 hours before serving. Serve with crackers.

MAKES 3 CUPS

ROQUEFORT SPREAD

3 ounces Roquefort cheese, softened
3 ounces cream cheese, softened
¼ cup butter or margarine, softened
¼ cup chopped walnuts
Crackers

In a bowl mix together the Roquefort cheese, cream cheese, and butter or margarine. Beat with an electric mixer until smooth. Pour into a serving bowl and sprinkle with the walnuts. Serve with crackers.

MAKES 2 CUPS

HOLIDAY CHEESE LOG

8 ounces cream cheese, softened
½ cup sour cream
¼ cup butter or margarine, softened
2 tablespoons finely chopped pimiento
1 tablespoon parsley flakes
1 teaspoon grated onion
1 cup finely chopped walnuts

In a medium bowl combine the cream cheese, sour cream, and butter or margarine. Beat with an electric mixer until fluffy. Stir in the pimiento, parsley flakes, and onion. Cover and chill for 2 hours. Place on wax paper and shape into a log. Coat with walnuts. Chill for at least 1 hour before serving.

MAKES 3 CUPS

BAKED BRIE WITH MANGO

1   8-ounce round Brie cheese
2   tablespoons raspberry preserves
¼   cup diced mango
1   tablespoon brown sugar
    Crackers

Preheat the oven to 400°. Place the Brie cheese in an 8-inch pie pan. Spread the raspberry preserves over the cheese and top with the mango and brown sugar. Bake for 10 to 12 minutes. Serve with crackers.

MAKES 2 CUPS

SUN-DRIED TOMATO PATÉ

¼ cup cottage cheese, drained

2 ounces goat cheese, softened

3 ounces sun-dried tomatoes, drained
and chopped

⅛ teaspoon thyme
French bread, toasted

2 teaspoons finely chopped fresh
parsley

In a blender purée the cottage cheese until smooth. In a medium bowl mix together the cottage cheese, goat cheese, tomatoes, and thyme. Serve on toasted French bread, topped with parsley.

MAKES 1½ CUPS

SOUPS
AND SALADS

ALMOND SOUP GRATINÉE

1	tablespoon butter or margarine, softened
4	slices French bread
2	cloves garlic, minced
1	cup blanched slivered almonds, toasted
6	cups vegetable stock
	Salt and pepper to taste
2	eggs, lightly beaten
1	cup shredded Gruyere cheese
	Paprika to taste

Preheat the oven to 350°. Butter both sides of the bread and place on a baking sheet. Bake for 10 minutes or until the bread is lightly browned. Turn and lightly brown the other side. Increase the oven temperature to 425°.

In a blender process the garlic and most of the almonds, reserving 1 tablespoon for garnish, until the nuts are very finely chopped. In a 3-quart saucepan place the nut mixture and add the vegetable stock. Bring to a boil, cover, and simmer for 15 minutes. Add the salt and pepper. Remove from the heat and add the eggs, stirring constantly, until smooth. Ladle the soup into 4 ovenproof bowls, and top with the toasted French bread slices. Garnish with the Gruyere cheese, reserved almonds, and paprika. Bake the soup for 10 minutes, then broil until the cheese is melted.

MAKES 4 SERVINGS

FRESH ASPARAGUS SOUP

1   pound fresh asparagus, trimmed
¾   cup chopped onion
1¾ cups vegetable stock
1   tablespoon butter or margarine
2   tablespoons all-purpose flour
1   teaspoon salt
⅛   teaspoon pepper
1   cup milk
½   cup plain yogurt
1   teaspoon lemon juice
¼   cup grated Parmesan cheese

In a saucepan place the asparagus and onion with ½ cup vegetable stock. Bring to a boil, reduce the heat, and let simmer until the vegetables are tender. Cut off several asparagus tips and set aside for garnish. In a blender purée the remaining vegetable mixture until smooth. In a medium saucepan melt the butter or margarine. Gradually add the flour, salt, and pepper, stirring constantly. Stir in the remaining vegetable stock and cook, stirring, until bubbles begin to form. Reduce the heat and add the vegetable purée and milk. Whisk the yogurt into the mixture, followed by the lemon juice. Stir until heated through. Garnish each serving with asparagus tips and Parmesan cheese.

MAKES 4 SERVINGS

BROCCOLI CHEESE SOUP

2 tablespoons butter or margarine
2 tablespoons chopped onion
3 tablespoons all-purpose flour
½ teaspoon salt
⅛ teaspoon pepper
2 cups milk
1 cup shredded American cheese
1½ cups vegetable stock
1 10-ounce package frozen chopped broccoli

In a large saucepan heat the butter or margarine and cook the onion until tender. Gradually stir in the flour, salt, and pepper. Add the milk and cook, stirring constantly, until thickened. Fold in the American cheese and stir until melted. In a separate pan bring the vegetable stock to a boil and add the broccoli. Cook until tender. Add the broccoli and vegetable stock to the cheese mixture, stirring until well blended.

MAKES 4 SERVINGS

CHEESY CAULIFLOWER SOUP

1 large cauliflower
1 medium potato, peeled and diced
1 medium carrot, chopped
3 cloves garlic, chopped
1½ cups chopped onion
1½ teaspoons salt
4 cups water
3 cups grated Cheddar cheese
¾ cup milk
1 teaspoon dill weed
½ teaspoon caraway seeds
  Pepper to taste

Break off about 2 cups of cauliflower florets, and steam until just tender. Set aside. Coarsely chop the remaining cauliflower. In a large saucepan place the chopped cauliflower, potato, carrot, garlic, onion, salt, and water. Bring to a boil, then reduce the heat and simmer until all of the vegetables are very tender. Pour the mixture into a blender, and purée until smooth. Transfer the mixture to a large pot. Add the reserved cauliflower florets, 2 cups of the Cheddar cheese, milk, dill, caraway seeds, and pepper, and cook until heated through. Garnish with the remaining cheese.

MAKES 6 TO 8 SERVINGS

GERMAN CHEESE SOUP

4 tablespoons butter or margarine
⅓ cup chopped green onion
¼ cup chopped carrot
¼ cup chopped cabbage
¼ cup all-purpose flour
3 cups vegetable stock
1 tablespoon Dijon mustard
2 cups half and half
2 cups shredded sharp Cheddar cheese

In a large saucepan melt the butter or margarine. Add the green onion, carrot, and cabbage. Cook and stir over medium-high heat until the onion and cabbage are tender. Stir in the flour and cook for 1 minute, stirring constantly. Continue stirring, add the vegetable stock and mustard, and bring to a low boil. Reduce the heat to low, cover, and simmer for 30 minutes.

In a small pan warm the half and half. Add the warm half and half and Cheddar cheese to the vegetable mixture. Stir until the soup is thoroughly heated and the cheese is melted.

MAKES 8 SERVINGS

THICK 'N' CREAMY CHEESE SOUP

½ cup butter or margarine
4 tablespoons all-purpose flour
4 cups milk
1½ cups grated carrots
1 cup chopped onion
2 cups chopped celery
2 cups shredded sharp Cheddar cheese
½ cup shredded Gouda cheese
1 2-ounce jar chopped pimientos
Salt and pepper to taste

In a large saucepan melt the butter or margarine. Gradually add the flour, stirring constantly, until the mixture is smooth. Add the milk, carrots, onion, celery, Cheddar cheese, Gouda cheese, and pimientos, and cook, stirring constantly, for 15 minutes or until the mixture is thickened and well blended. Season with salt and pepper.

MAKES 8 SERVINGS

CHEESE TORTELLINI SOUP

1   7-ounce package cheese-filled
    tortellini
2½ cups water
2   tablespoons rice wine vinegar
2   tablespoons soy sauce
1   10-ounce can condensed vegetable
    stock
1½ teaspoons ginger
2   cups sliced bok choy
2   green onions, sliced
1   cup enoki mushrooms

Cook the tortellini according to the package directions and drain.
In a large saucepan heat the water, vinegar, soy sauce, vegetable
stock, and ginger. Bring to a boil; reduce the heat. Cut the bok
choy stems, reserving the leaves for later use. Stir in the bok choy
stems and green onions, and simmer for 15 minutes. Stir in the
bok choy leaves and mushrooms. Cook until the leaves are just
wilted.

MAKES 4 SERVINGS

SUMPTUOUS LEEK SOUP

¼ cup butter or margarine
2 cups sliced leeks
2 cloves garlic, minced
4 tablespoons all-purpose flour
¼ teaspoon pepper
2 cups half and half
4 cups vegetable stock
1 cup shredded Jarlsberg cheese
1 cup shredded Swiss cheese
1 cup pine nuts, toasted
2 tablespoons chopped fresh chives

In a large saucepan heat the butter or margarine over medium heat. Cook the leeks and garlic in the butter or margarine for about 2 minutes. Gradually stir in the flour and pepper. Stir in the half and half and vegetable stock. Bring to a boil, and boil for 1 minute, stirring constantly. Add the Jarlsberg cheese, Swiss cheese, and pine nuts, and stir until the cheese is melted and the soup is hot. Sprinkle with chives.

MAKES 6 TO 8 SERVINGS

GARDEN FRESH MINESTRONE

3	tablespoons olive oil
1	medium onion, chopped
2	cloves garlic, minced
8	cups vegetable stock
1	15-ounce can kidney beans, undrained
1	cup chopped celery
2	cups green beans, cut into 1-inch pieces
1	medium carrot, chopped
1	medium bell pepper, chopped
1	small zucchini, chopped
1	teaspoon basil
1	teaspoon oregano
1	medium tomato, diced
½	cup tomato paste
½	cup elbow macaroni
	Salt and pepper to taste
1	cup grated Parmesan cheese

In a large pot heat the olive oil and cook the onion and garlic over medium heat, stirring occasionally, for 5 minutes. Add the vegetable stock, kidney beans with juice, celery, green beans, carrot, bell pepper, zucchini, basil, and oregano, and bring to a boil. Reduce the heat, cover, and simmer for 30 minutes.

Stir in the tomato, tomato paste, and macaroni, and continue simmering for 15 minutes or until the macaroni is tender. Season with salt and pepper, and garnish with Parmesan cheese.

MAKES 8 SERVINGS

SWISS ONION SOUP

2 tablespoons butter or margarine
2 medium onions, thinly sliced
1 clove garlic, minced
1½ teaspoons salt
2 teaspoons dry mustard
1 tablespoon all-purpose flour
2 cups water
1 teaspoon horseradish
1½ cups milk, warmed
2 cups grated Swiss cheese
Pepper to taste
Croutons

In a large pot melt the butter or margarine. Add the onions, garlic, salt, and dry mustard, and cook over medium heat for 8 to 10 minutes, or until the onions are very soft. Gradually sprinkle in the flour, stirring constantly, and mix well. Add the water and horseradish. Stir and cook for 5 more minutes. Add the warm milk and Swiss cheese, stirring constantly for several minutes, until the soup is smooth and well blended. Season with pepper, and garnish with croutons.

MAKES 6 TO 8 SERVINGS

DIVINE POTATO SOUP

6   medium potatoes, peeled and cubed
6   cups water
1½ cups chopped celery
1   cup chopped onion
1   12-ounce can condensed milk
½   cup butter or margarine
    Salt and pepper to taste
1   teaspoon garlic salt
1   tablespoon parsley flakes
1½ cups grated Cheddar cheese
    Crackers

In a large saucepan boil the potatoes in the water for 30 minutes or until just tender. Add the celery and onion, and cook for 10 minutes longer. Gradually add the condensed milk and butter or margarine, stirring constantly, until smooth. Season with salt and pepper, garlic salt, and parsley flakes. Simmer for 10 minutes, or until ready to serve. Gently fold in the Cheddar cheese, and serve with crackers.

MAKES 6 TO 8 SERVINGS

SAVORY PUMPKIN SOUP

5	cups pumpkin purée
2	cups vegetable stock
2	cups whipping cream
½	teaspoon garlic powder
½	teaspoon onion powder
4	ounces elbow macaroni
½	teaspoon pumpkin pie spice
½	cup minced fresh parsley
¼	cup chopped fresh cilantro
¼	cup butter or margarine, softened
½	cup plain yogurt
½	cup sour cream
¼	cup shredded mozzarella cheese
¼	cup almonds, toasted

In a large saucepan mix the pumpkin, vegetable stock, cream, garlic powder, and onion powder. Bring to a boil. Stir in the macaroni, and cook for 10 to 12 minutes, or until the macaroni is tender but firm. Reduce the heat to low. Stir in the pumpkin pie spice, parsley, and cilantro. Gradually stir in the butter or margarine, yogurt, and sour cream. Continue stirring, and add the mozzarella cheese. Serve topped with almonds.

MAKES 8 TO 10 SERVINGS

SOUTH OF THE BORDER SOUP

4	corn tortillas
⅓	cup vegetable oil
1½	tablespoons butter or margarine
⅓	cup pine nuts
½	cup chopped walnuts
1	small onion, chopped
1	clove garlic, minced
6	cups vegetable stock
2	cups butternut squash, peeled and diced
1	10-ounce package frozen corn
1	large avocado, peeled and diced
2	cups shredded Monterey Jack cheese

Cut the tortillas into 6 equal wedges. In a medium skillet heat the vegetable oil on medium-high heat and fry the tortilla pieces in vegetable oil until very lightly browned. Drain and cool on paper towels.

In a large saucepan melt ½ tablespoon of the butter or margarine over medium heat. Add the pine nuts and walnuts and cook, stirring, until golden, about 2 minutes. Remove the nuts and set aside. In the same pan melt the remaining tablespoon of butter or margarine, and sauté the onion and garlic until the onion is golden. Add the vegetable stock and squash and bring to a boil. Reduce the heat, cover, and simmer for 10 to 15 minutes or until the squash is tender. Add the corn and cook for 5 more minutes. Ladle the soup into individual bowls, and top with avocado, nuts, Monterey Jack cheese, and tortilla pieces.

MAKES 6 SERVINGS

CREAMY TOMATO SOUP

2   tablespoons butter or margarine
1   medium onion, chopped
2   14-ounce cans diced tomatoes, undrained
2   10-ounce cans condensed tomato soup
1½ cups milk
1   teaspoon sugar
½   teaspoon basil
½   teaspoon paprika
¼   teaspoon garlic powder
8   ounces cream cheese, cubed
    Croutons

In a large saucepan heat the butter or margarine, and sauté the onion until tender. Stir in the tomatoes, tomato soup, milk, sugar, basil, paprika, and garlic powder. Cover and simmer for 10 minutes. Add the cream cheese, stirring constantly until melted. Top each serving with croutons.

MAKES 6 TO 8 SERVINGS

VEGETARIAN CAESAR

Dressing:

1	clove garlic, minced
⅓	cup olive oil
3	tablespoons lemon juice
1	teaspoon Worcestershire sauce
¼	teaspoon salt
¼	teaspoon dry mustard
1	tablespoon mayonnaise
2	heads Romaine lettuce, rinsed and torn into pieces
1	cup garlic-flavored croutons
½	cup grated Parmesan cheese

In a medium bowl whisk together the garlic, olive oil, lemon juice, Worcestershire sauce, salt, dry mustard, and mayonnaise. In a large bowl mix the lettuce, croutons, and Parmesan cheese. Add the dressing and toss well.

MAKES 8 SERVINGS

CALIFORNIA SALAD

Dressing:
1   avocado, peeled and pitted
1   tablespoon lemon juice
½   cup mayonnaise
¼   teaspoon hot pepper sauce
¼   cup olive oil
1   clove garlic, minced
½   teaspoon salt

1   head Romaine lettuce, rinsed and
    torn into pieces
1   cup shredded Cheddar cheese
2   tomatoes, diced
2   green onions, chopped
½   cup sliced black olives
1   cup coarsely crushed corn chips

In a blender combine the avocado, lemon juice, mayonnaise, hot pepper sauce, olive oil, garlic, and salt, and purée until smooth. In a large bowl toss together the lettuce, Cheddar cheese, tomatoes, green onions, olives, and corn chips. Just before serving, drizzle with dressing and toss lightly.

MAKES 6 SERVINGS

CASHEW TOSSED SALAD

Dressing:

⅓	cup white vinegar
¾	cup sugar
2	teaspoons mustard
1	teaspoon grated onion
	Salt to taste
1	cup vegetable oil
1	teaspoon poppy seeds
1	head Romaine lettuce, rinsed and torn into pieces
1	cup salted cashews
4	ounces Swiss cheese, cut into thin strips

In a blender combine the vinegar, sugar, mustard, onion, and salt, and purée until smooth. Gradually add the oil, puréeing until well blended. Transfer to a small bowl, and stir in the poppy seeds. In a large bowl combine the romaine lettuce, cashews, and Swiss cheese. Top with dressing to serve.

MAKES 6 SERVINGS

GREEK SALAD

3 cups bite-size pieces spinach
¼ cup crumbled feta cheese
2 tablespoons sliced black olives
2 medium tomatoes, chopped
1 medium cucumber, chopped
½ cup diced onion
½ cup chopped green bell pepper

Dressing:
1½ tablespoons olive oil
1 tablespoon red wine vinegar
1 tablespoon lemon juice
¾ teaspoon oregano

In a large bowl combine the spinach, feta cheese, olives, tomatoes, cucumber, onion, and bell pepper, and set aside. In a small bowl whisk together the olive oil, vinegar, lemon juice, and oregano. Pour over the spinach mixture and toss well.

MAKES 6 SERVINGS

HARVEST SALAD

1 bunch spinach, rinsed and torn into pieces
½ cup chopped walnuts, toasted
½ cup dried cranberries
½ cup crumbled blue cheese
2 tomatoes, chopped
1 avocado, peeled and chopped
1 small onion, thinly sliced

Dressing:
2 tablespoons red raspberry jam
2 tablespoons red wine vinegar
⅓ cup olive oil
Salt and pepper to taste

In a large bowl toss together the spinach, walnuts, cranberries, blue cheese, tomatoes, avocado, and onion. In a small bowl whisk together the jam, vinegar, olive oil, salt, and pepper. Pour the dressing over the salad immediately before serving, and toss lightly.

MAKES 6 SERVINGS

ROQUEFORT AND TOASTED WALNUT SALAD

1   small head radicchio, rinsed and torn into pieces

1   head Bibb lettuce, rinsed and torn into pieces

½   cup crumbled Roquefort cheese

½   cup chopped fresh chives

⅓   cup coarsely chopped walnuts, toasted

Dressing:

⅓   cup olive oil

2   tablespoons lemon juice

1   clove garlic

⅛   teaspoon salt

Pepper to taste

¼   cup chopped walnuts, toasted

In a large bowl mix together the radicchio, Bibb lettuce, Roquefort cheese, chives, and ⅓ cup walnuts, and set aside. In a blender combine the olive oil, lemon juice, garlic, salt, pepper, and ¼ cup walnuts. Purée until smooth. Pour over the lettuce mixture and toss.

MAKES 6 SERVINGS

SPRING SALAD

Dressing:

½ cup safflower oil

⅓ cup white vinegar

¼ cup walnut oil

1 tablespoon Dijon mustard
   Salt and pepper to taste

1 head Boston lettuce, rinsed and torn
   into pieces

1 head Romaine lettuce, rinsed and
   torn into pieces

1 bunch escarole, rinsed and torn into
   pieces

¾ cup walnut halves, toasted

¾ cup grated Cheddar cheese

In a small bowl combine the safflower oil, vinegar, walnut oil, mustard, salt, and pepper, and mix well. In a large bowl combine the Boston lettuce, Romaine lettuce, escarole, walnuts, and Cheddar cheese, and toss with dressing before serving.

MAKES 8 SERVINGS

SPINACH CHEESE SALAD

1   bunch spinach, rinsed and torn into
    pieces
1   head iceberg lettuce, rinsed and torn
    into pieces
2   cups cottage cheese
3   cups grated Swiss cheese
1   red onion, thinly sliced

Dressing:
1   cup olive oil
½   cup sugar
½   cup cider vinegar
1   teaspoon salt
1   teaspoon dry mustard

In a large bowl combine the spinach, lettuce, cottage cheese, 2
cups Swiss cheese, and onion. In a small bowl whisk together the
olive oil, sugar, vinegar, salt, and dry mustard. Pour over the
spinach mixture and toss to coat. Top with the remaining Swiss
cheese.

MAKES 6 SERVINGS

STRAWBERRY SPINACH TOSS

5   cups bite-size pieces spinach
1   cup sliced strawberries
⅓   cup chopped pecans, toasted
½   cup sliced Gouda cheese

Dressing:
2   tablespoons lime juice
2   tablespoons honey
1   tablespoon vegetable oil
½   teaspoon ginger

In a large bowl combine the spinach, strawberries, pecans, and Gouda cheese. In a small bowl whisk together the lime juice, honey, vegetable oil, and ginger, and pour over the salad. Toss lightly before serving.

MAKES 6 SERVINGS

TRUE BLUE SALAD

Dressing:
1 cup mayonnaise
1 cup sour cream
½ cup crumbled blue cheese
¼ teaspoon garlic salt
¼ teaspoon parsley flakes

6 cups mixed greens
2 medium tomatoes, chopped
½ cup chopped walnuts

In a medium bowl whisk together the mayonnaise, sour cream, blue cheese, garlic salt, and parsley flakes until thoroughly blended. Chill for at least 2 hours.

In a large bowl toss the mixed greens, tomatoes, and walnuts together, and serve with the dressing.

MAKES 4 TO 6 SERVINGS

ZESTY MARINADE SALAD

¼ cup olive oil
2 teaspoons basil
½ teaspoon salt
⅛ teaspoon pepper
⅛ teaspoon paprika
2 teaspoons Dijon mustard
5 teaspoons white wine vinegar
3 cups sliced fresh mushrooms
2 green onions, thinly sliced
⅔ cup coarsely chopped walnuts
1 cup crumbled blue cheese
1 head Romaine lettuce, rinsed and
torn into pieces
10 cherry tomatoes, halved

In a large salad bowl whisk together the olive oil, basil, salt, pepper, paprika, mustard, and vinegar. Add the mushrooms and green onions; let stand at room temperature at least 30 minutes to marinate.

Add the walnuts, blue cheese, lettuce, and cherry tomatoes, and toss lightly.

MAKES 6 SERVINGS

APPLE-CHEESE COLESLAW

½   cup sour cream
¼   cup mayonnaise
1   teaspoon sugar
½   teaspoon dry mustard
½   teaspoon seasoned salt
⅛   teaspoon pepper
3   cups finely shredded cabbage
1   medium carrot, shredded
1   apple, diced
¼   cup crumbled blue cheese

In a medium bowl mix together the sour cream, mayonnaise, sugar, dry mustard, seasoned salt, and pepper. In a large bowl combine the cabbage, carrot, apple, and blue cheese. Add the sour cream mixture, and mix well.

MAKES 8 SERVINGS

APPLE-CINNAMON DELIGHT

1 cup hot water
⅓ cup small red cinnamon candies
1 3-ounce package lemon gelatin mix
½ cup cold water
¾ cup applesauce
8 ounces cream cheese
¼ cup chopped pecans
¼ cup finely chopped celery
3 tablespoons mayonnaise

In a medium bowl mix together the hot water and cinnamon candies, stirring rapidly until the candy is dissolved. Stir in the gelatin mix. When the gelatin is dissolved, add the cold water and applesauce. Pour half of the mixture into an 8-inch square pan, and chill until firm. Let the reserved mixture stand at room temperature. In a medium bowl blend the cream cheese, pecans, celery, and mayonnaise. Spread into the pan over the firm gelatin. Pour the remaining gelatin mixture over top, and chill until firm.

MAKES 6 SERVINGS

CAPRESE SALAD

2 large tomatoes, sliced
8 ounces mozzarella cheese, sliced
1 bunch fresh basil leaves, sliced
3 tablespoons olive oil
2 tablespoons balsamic vinegar
Salt and pepper to taste

Arrange the tomato slices on a serving platter. Top with the mozzarella cheese slices and basil. In a small bowl whisk together the oil and vinegar. Drizzle over the cheese slices. Season with salt and pepper.

MAKES 6 SERVINGS

GOLDEN MANDARIN SALAD

1 apple
1 teaspoon lemon juice
1 tablespoon olive oil
1 11-ounce can mandarin oranges, drained
4 carrots, grated
¼ cup chopped pitted dates
1 cup shredded Cheddar cheese
Salt and pepper to taste

Grate the apple into a medium bowl, and immediately add the lemon juice and olive oil. Mix in the oranges, carrots, dates, Cheddar cheese, salt, and pepper, and toss well.

MAKES 4 SERVINGS

WALDORF SALAD SUPREME

1   8-ounce can pineapple chunks,
    undrained
1   cup plain yogurt
¼   cup mayonnaise
¼   teaspoon cinnamon
2   medium apples, coarsely chopped
1   medium stalk celery, chopped
⅓   cup chopped pecans, toasted
1   cup small seedless grapes
1   cup diced Cheddar cheese

Drain the pineapple chunks, reserving the juice. In a small bowl whisk together the pineapple juice, yogurt, mayonnaise, and cinnamon. In a large mixing bowl combine the pineapple chunks, apples, celery, pecans, grapes, and Cheddar cheese. Stir in the yogurt mixture, and mix well.

MAKES 4 TO 6 SERVINGS

WARM PEAR SALAD WITH RASPBERRY VINAIGRETTE

2 large pears, sliced

4 cups mixed salad greens, torn into pieces

4 slices red onion, separated into rings

½ cup crumbled blue cheese

2 tablespoons sunflower seeds

Raspberry Vinaigrette:

½ cup olive oil

⅓ cup honey

⅓ cup white wine vinegar

1 tablespoon Dijon mustard

1 teaspoon lemon juice

¾ cup fresh raspberries

¼ teaspoon salt

In a medium skillet sauté the pear slices for 2 to 3 minutes on each side until tender. Arrange the salad greens, pears, onion, blue cheese, and sunflower seeds on individual plates. In a blender combine all of the ingredients for the raspberry vinaigrette; purée until smooth. Drizzle the vinaigrette over the salads before serving.

MAKES 6 SERVINGS

BLUE CHEESE POTATO SALAD

2½ pounds small red potatoes, cooked
   and cubed

¾ cup chopped green onion

¾ cup chopped celery

¾ cup sour cream

¼ cup mayonnaise

2   tablespoons minced fresh parsley

1   tablespoon white wine vinegar

1½ teaspoons salt

¼ teaspoon pepper

¼ teaspoon celery seed

½ cup crumbled blue cheese

In a large bowl toss the potatoes, green onion, and celery. In a small bowl combine the sour cream, mayonnaise, parsley, vinegar, salt, pepper, and celery seed, and mix well. Pour over the potato mixture, and toss to coat. Sprinkle with the blue cheese and toss lightly. Cover and refrigerate for several hours before serving.

MAKES 8 SERVINGS

ITALIAN PASTA SALAD

7 ounces spiral macaroni
½ cup sliced black olives
2 medium tomatoes, chopped
1 green bell pepper, chopped
2 green onions, chopped
½ cup white wine vinegar
2 tablespoons water
2 tablespoons olive oil
½ teaspoon salt
½ teaspoon sesame oil
1 clove garlic, minced
½ cup Parmesan cheese

Cook the macaroni according to the package directions, rinse with cold water, and drain. In a large bowl combine the macaroni, olives, tomatoes, bell pepper, and green onions; mix well. In a small bowl whisk together the vinegar, water, olive oil, salt, sesame oil, and garlic. Pour over the macaroni mixture, and toss well. Stir in the Parmesan cheese. Cover and refrigerate for at least 30 minutes before serving.

MAKES 6 SERVINGS

ASPARAGUS PARMESAN SALAD

8   ounces asparagus, cut into 2-inch pieces
1   tomato, chopped
2   tablespoons thinly sliced green onion
3   tablespoons plain yogurt
1   tablespoon grated Parmesan cheese
1   teaspoon mustard

Steam the asparagus until just tender and let cool. Chill for 30 minutes or until thoroughly cooled.

In a medium salad bowl combine the asparagus, tomato, and green onion. In a small bowl whisk together the yogurt, Parmesan cheese, and mustard. Add to the vegetable mixture, and toss until well coated.

MAKES 4 TO 6 SERVINGS

MEDITERRANEAN WHEAT SALAD

8 ounces bulgur wheat

1¼ cups boiling water

4 tablespoons olive oil

3 tablespoons lemon juice

2 tablespoons chopped fresh mint

3 tablespoons chopped fresh coriander

2 medium onions, chopped

2 cloves garlic, chopped

1½ cups chopped cucumber

2 cups crumbled feta cheese

1 lime, cut into wedges

In a large bowl combine the bulgur wheat and boiling water. Soak for 30 minutes, stirring occasionally with a fork, until the water is absorbed.

In a small bowl whisk together the oil and lemon juice. Pour the oil mixture over the wheat. Add the mint and coriander, and mix well. Stir in the onions, garlic, cucumber, and feta cheese. Cover and chill for at least 45 minutes before serving. Garnish with lime wedges.

MAKES 6 SERVINGS

MARINATED PEPPERS AND OLIVES

3	large bell peppers
2	tablespoons olive oil
1	tablespoon chopped fresh parsley
1	tablespoon lemon juice
1	tablespoon lime juice
¼	teaspoon salt
⅛	teaspoon oregano
⅛	teaspoon basil
⅛	teaspoon sage leaves
⅛	teaspoon pepper
1	clove garlic, chopped
1	cup pitted whole black olives
1	cup cubed feta cheese

Place the bell peppers on a lightly oiled baking sheet and broil, turning occasionally, until lightly browned. Place the peppers in a plastic bag and close tightly. Let stand for 20 minutes.

Cut the peppers into eighths and set aside. In a small bowl combine the olive oil, parsley, lemon juice, lime juice, salt, oregano, basil, sage, pepper, and garlic, and mix well. In a medium bowl combine the bell peppers, olives, and feta cheese, and top with the spice mixture. Cover and refrigerate at least 4 hours, stirring occasionally.

MAKES 6 SERVINGS

PROTEIN DREAM SALAD

2   large heads Boston lettuce, rinsed and torn into pieces

1½ cups fresh whole mushrooms

1   medium carrot, sliced

½   cup Spanish-style peanuts

3   tablespoons chopped fresh parsley

2   tablespoons wheat germ

2   tablespoons sunflower seeds

2   tablespoons unsweetened granola cereal

½   cup bean sprouts

½   cup shredded Monterey Jack cheese

¾   cup plain yogurt

3   tablespoons olive oil

1½ tablespoons lemon juice

1   avocado, peeled and sliced

In a large serving bowl mix the lettuce, mushrooms, carrot, and peanuts. Sprinkle in the parsley, wheat germ, sunflower seeds, granola, sprouts, and Monterey Jack cheese. In a small bowl whisk together the yogurt, olive oil, and lemon juice. Pour over the salad and toss gently. Garnish with avocado slices.

MAKES 6 SERVINGS

MAIN DISHES

ARTICHOKE PIE

1 tablespoon olive oil

1 clove garlic, minced

2 6-ounce jars artichoke hearts, drained

½ cup Italian-seasoned dry breadcrumbs

½ cup grated Parmesan cheese

1 9-inch pie crust, unbaked

2 cups shredded mozzarella cheese

Preheat the oven to 350°. In a large skillet heat the oil over medium heat. Sauté the garlic until it starts to brown. Stir in the artichoke hearts and cook for 10 minutes, stirring occasionally. Mix in the breadcrumbs and Parmesan cheese and cook until the cheese is melted. Transfer the artichoke mixture to the pie crust. Top with mozzarella cheese. Bake for 45 minutes or until the crust begins to brown.

MAKES 6 TO 8 SERVINGS

ASPARAGUS CASSEROLE

1   15-ounce can baby peas, drained
1   8-ounce can sliced water chestnuts,
    drained
1   10-ounce can condensed cream of
    mushroom soup
1   15-ounce can asparagus, drained
2   cups shredded Cheddar cheese
1   cup butter or margarine
8   slices white bread, crusts removed
    and cut into ½-inch strips
1   cup grated Parmesan cheese

Preheat the oven to 350°. In a medium bowl mix together the peas, water chestnuts, and cream of mushroom soup. Place the asparagus in the bottom of a medium casserole dish and top with the pea mixture. Sprinkle with Cheddar cheese. In a skillet melt the butter or margarine over medium heat. Soak the bread strips in the melted butter or margarine and arrange evenly in the casserole dish on top of the Cheddar cheese. Sprinkle with Parmesan cheese, and bake for 35 minutes or until bubbly.

MAKES 8 SERVINGS

BROCCOLI CHEESE BAKE

1   10-ounce can condensed cream of
    mushroom soup
¾   cup mayonnaise
¼   cup finely chopped onion
2   10-ounce packages frozen chopped
    broccoli
2   cups shredded sharp Cheddar cheese
⅛   teaspoon paprika
1   cup crushed butter crackers

Preheat the oven to 350°. Grease a 9 x 13-inch baking dish. In a medium bowl stir together the cream of mushroom soup, mayonnaise, and onion. Break up the frozen broccoli and place it in a large mixing bowl. Stir in the soup mixture, Cheddar cheese, and paprika, and mix well. Spread the mixture into the prepared baking dish and top with cracker crumbs. Bake for 50 to 55 minutes or until the cheese is thoroughly melted.

MAKES 6 TO 8 SERVINGS

CASINO ROYALE CASSEROLE

1	10-ounce package frozen chopped broccoli
½	cup sliced fresh mushrooms
2	tablespoons butter or margarine
2	tablespoons all-purpose flour
½	teaspoon salt
¼	teaspoon pepper
¼	teaspoon nutmeg
2	cups milk
1½	cups grated Swiss cheese
2	teaspoons lemon juice
¼	cup grated Parmesan cheese
1	12-ounce package refrigerated biscuit dough

Preheat the oven to 375°. In a medium saucepan boil the broccoli and mushrooms for 4 to 5 minutes, or until just tender. Drain and set aside. In a medium saucepan melt the butter or margarine. Blend in the flour, salt, pepper, and nutmeg, and cook, stirring, for 1 to 2 minutes over medium-low heat. Gradually add the milk, stirring constantly, until thickened. Remove from the heat and stir in the Swiss cheese. Add the lemon juice, broccoli, and mushrooms. Pour the mixture into a 9 x 13-inch baking dish and top with Parmesan cheese. Place the rounds of biscuit dough side by side on top of the cheese. Bake for about 20 minutes or until the biscuits are golden brown.

MAKES 6 SERVINGS

CAMEMBERT SOUFFLÉ

¼ cup grated Parmesan cheese

4 tablespoons butter or margarine

¼ teaspoon nutmeg

⅛ teaspoon ground red pepper

3 tablespoons all-purpose flour

1½ cups milk

2 teaspoons Dijon mustard

2 tablespoons dry sherry

4 ounces ripe Camembert cheese, rind removed

1¼ cups Gruyere cheese

4 eggs, separated

¼ teaspoon cream of tartar

¼ teaspoon salt

Preheat the oven to 375°. Butter a 2-quart soufflé dish or baking dish. Sprinkle the dish with the Parmesan cheese and set aside. In a medium saucepan melt the butter or margarine over medium heat. Add the nutmeg and red pepper. Blend in the flour and cook, stirring constantly, until bubbly. Gradually pour in the milk and continue stirring until the sauce thickens. Add the mustard, sherry, Camembert cheese, and Gruyere cheese. Stir just until the cheeses are melted. In a small bowl beat the egg yolks. Gradually stir ¼ cup of the cheese sauce into the egg yolks, then stir the mixture back into the cheese sauce. Return to the heat and cook, stirring, for 1 minute. In a large bowl combine the egg whites, cream of tartar, and salt. Beat until short, moist peaks form. Fold ¼ cup of the beaten egg whites into the cheese sauce. Slowly fold the sauce into the remaining egg whites. Pour into the prepared baking dish. Bake for 35 to 40 minutes or until the top is browned.

MAKES 6 SERVINGS

CHEESE LOAF

4 cups cottage cheese

4 eggs, beaten

¼ cup vegetable oil

1 envelope dry onion soup mix

1 cup finely chopped walnuts

1½ cups cornflakes cereal

Preheat the oven to 350°. Lightly oil a loaf pan. In a large bowl mix together the cottage cheese, eggs, oil, onion soup mix, walnuts, and cornflakes. Pour the mixture into the prepared pan. Bake for 35 to 40 minutes.

MAKES 8 SERVINGS

EGGPLANT PARMESAN

1	medium eggplant, peeled and cut into ¼-inch slices
	Cooking spray
1	cup marinara sauce
⅓	cup grated Parmesan cheese
2	teaspoons vegetable oil
¼	cup Italian-seasoned dry breadcrumbs
1½	cups shredded mozzarella cheese

Spray both sides of each eggplant slice with cooking spray, and place in a broiler pan. Broil the slices for about 10 minutes, turning once. Meanwhile, in a saucepan heat the marinara sauce over medium heat and cook for about 2 minutes, stirring occasionally. Remove from the heat and cover. In a small bowl mix together the Parmesan cheese, vegetable oil, and breadcrumbs. Sprinkle the Parmesan cheese mixture and 1 cup of the mozzarella cheese over the eggplant slices. Broil for about 1 minute or until the cheese is melted. Top with the marinara sauce and remaining mozzarella cheese before serving.

MAKES 6 SERVINGS

GARDEN CASSEROLE

¼ cup vegetable oil

1 large eggplant, peeled and cubed

2 medium onions, finely chopped

2 cloves garlic, minced

2 medium zucchini, sliced

5 tomatoes, chopped

1 cup sliced celery

¼ cup chopped fresh parsley

¼ cup chopped fresh basil

2 teaspoons salt

½ teaspoon pepper

½ cup grated Romano cheese

1 cup Italian-seasoned dry breadcrumbs

2 tablespoons butter or margarine, melted

1 cup shredded mozzarella cheese

Preheat the oven to 375°. Grease a 9 x 13-inch baking dish. In a medium skillet heat the vegetable oil and sauté the eggplant until lightly browned, about 5 minutes. Add the onions, garlic, and zucchini, and cook for 3 minutes. Add the tomatoes, celery, parsley, basil, salt, and pepper, and bring to a boil. Reduce the heat, cover, and simmer for 10 minutes. Remove from the heat and stir in the Romano cheese. Pour the mixture into the prepared baking dish. Combine the breadcrumbs and butter or margarine, and sprinkle over the casserole mixture. Bake for 15 minutes. Sprinkle with mozzarella cheese. Bake for an additional 5 minutes or until the cheese is melted.

MAKES 10 SERVINGS

MANSION CASSEROLE

1	14-ounce can green beans, drained
1	11-ounce can whole kernel corn, drained
1	10-ounce can condensed cream of celery soup
¾	cup sour cream
½	cup chopped onion
½	cup chopped celery
½	cup ricotta cheese
⅔	cup crushed butter crackers
½	cup slivered almonds

Preheat the oven to 350°. Lightly oil a 9 x 13-inch baking dish. In a large bowl mix together the green beans, corn, cream of celery soup, sour cream, onion, celery, and ricotta cheese. Pour the mixture into the prepared baking dish. Top with the cracker crumbs, followed by the almonds. Bake for 45 minutes.

MAKES 6 SERVINGS

MOUSSAKA

¼ cup dry breadcrumbs

⅓ cup olive oil

2 large eggplants, peeled and sliced

3 medium potatoes, sliced

4 tablespoons butter or margarine

2 large onions, chopped

½ cup chopped fresh parsley

1 cup tomato sauce

⅓ cup all-purpose flour

2 cups milk

2 eggs, separated

¼ cup grated Romano cheese

¼ teaspoon nutmeg

Preheat the oven to 350°. Grease a 9 x 13-inch baking dish and dust with breadcrumbs. In a large skillet heat the olive oil and brown the eggplants and potatoes. Drain on paper towels and set aside. In a skillet heat 1 tablespoon butter or margarine and sauté the onion until brown. Add the parsley and tomato sauce and simmer for 10 minutes. Place one-third of the eggplant and potato mixture into the prepared baking dish, followed with one-third of the tomato sauce mixture. Repeat the layers. In a saucepan melt the remaining butter or margarine over low heat. Gradually add the flour, stirring constantly. Slowly add the milk to the flour mixture and cook, stirring constantly, until thickened. In a bowl beat the egg yolks. Stir in the Romano cheese and nutmeg. Add the cheese mixture to the milk sauce. Beat the egg whites until stiff and fold into the sauce. Pour the sauce over the eggplant-potato layers. Bake for 45 to 55 minutes or until golden brown.

MAKES 10 SERVINGS

MUSHROOM-BROCCOLI STROGANOFF

2 tablespoons butter or margarine
1 large onion, chopped
3 cups sliced fresh mushrooms
2 tablespoons lemon juice
½ teaspoon salt
½ teaspoon basil
1 cup sour cream
1 cup shredded Monterey Jack cheese
1 cup shredded Cheddar cheese
1 pound broccoli florets
12 ounces spinach noodles
⅓ cup sunflower seeds

Preheat the oven to 350°. In a large skillet melt the butter or margarine over medium heat. Add the onion and mushrooms and cook, stirring occasionally, for about 8 minutes or until soft. Remove from the heat and stir in the lemon juice, salt, basil, sour cream, half of the Monterey Jack cheese, and half of the Cheddar cheese. Mix until well blended and set aside. Steam the broccoli for about 5 minutes or until just tender. Cook the noodles according to the package directions and drain. In a large bowl combine the cheese mixture, noodles, and broccoli. Pour into a 9 x 13-inch baking dish and bake, covered, for 30 to 35 minutes. Sprinkle with the remaining cheese and sunflower seeds, and bake, uncovered, for 5 more minutes or until the cheese is melted.

MAKES 8 SERVINGS

SPINACH RICOTTA PIE

1	teaspoon butter or margarine
1	cup minced onion
3	cups finely chopped spinach
½	teaspoon salt
	Pepper to taste
1	teaspoon basil
16	ounces ricotta cheese
2	eggs, beaten
3	tablespoons all-purpose flour
½	cup grated Asiago cheese
1	9-inch pie crust, unbaked
	Paprika to taste

Preheat the oven to 375°. In a medium skillet melt the butter or margarine over medium heat. Add the onion, and sauté for 5 minutes. Add the spinach, salt, pepper, and basil, and cook, stirring, until the spinach is wilted. Remove from the heat. In a large bowl combine the spinach mixture, ricotta cheese, eggs, flour, and Asiago cheese, and mix well. Pour into the unbaked pie crust, and dust generously with paprika. Bake for 40 to 45 minutes.

MAKES 4 TO 6 SERVINGS

THREE-ONION PIE

2 cups dry breadcrumbs

2 tablespoons safflower oil

1 large yellow onion, chopped

1 large red onion, quartered

2 large leeks, chopped

2 tablespoons dry white wine

2 eggs, beaten

3 tablespoons chopped fresh parsley

1 tablespoon chopped fresh dill weed

1 teaspoon tarragon

1½ cups feta cheese

½ teaspoon pepper

1 medium tomato, thinly sliced

Preheat the oven to 350°. Lightly grease an 8-inch square baking dish and line the bottom evenly with three-fourths of the breadcrumbs. In a large skillet heat the safflower oil. Add the yellow and red onion, and sauté over medium heat for 5 minutes. Stir in the leeks and white wine. Sauté for another 15 minutes, stirring frequently, until the onions are golden and the leeks are tender. Remove from the heat. In a large mixing bowl combine the beaten eggs with 2 tablespoons of the parsley, the dill, tarragon, feta cheese, and pepper. Stir in the onion mixture. Pour the mixture into the prepared baking dish. Ring the outside edge of the pie with tomato slices, and sprinkle the remaining parsley in the center. Sprinkle the remaining breadcrumbs over the top of the pie and bake for 40 to 45 minutes or until golden.

MAKES 6 SERVINGS

VEGETABLE RATATOUILLE

2 tablespoons olive oil
1 medium onion, chopped
2 cloves garlic, minced
1 green bell pepper, thinly sliced
1 red bell pepper, thinly sliced
1 medium zucchini, thinly sliced
1 medium eggplant, peeled and cubed
3 tablespoons minced fresh basil
1 26-ounce jar marinara sauce
½ cup grated Parmesan cheese

Preheat the oven to 400°. In a large skillet heat 1 tablespoon of olive oil over medium heat. Add the onion, garlic, green and red peppers, zucchini, and eggplant. Sauté until the vegetables are tender. Add the basil and marinara sauce, and simmer for 5 minutes over low heat, stirring occasionally. Pour the mixture into a shallow baking dish, and sprinkle with Parmesan cheese. Bake for 25 to 30 minutes or until bubbly.

MAKES 6 TO 8 SERVINGS

YELLOW SQUASH CASSEROLE

4   cups sliced yellow squash
½   cup chopped onion
1   cup water
1   cup shredded Cheddar cheese
1¼ cups crushed butter crackers
2   eggs, beaten
¾   cup milk
¼   cup butter or margarine, melted
    Salt and pepper to taste

Preheat the oven to 400°. In a large skillet place the squash, onion, and water. Cover and cook over medium heat for about 5 minutes, or until tender. Drain and transfer to a medium bowl. In a small bowl mix together the Cheddar cheese and cracker crumbs. Stir half of the cheese mixture into the cooked squash. In another small bowl mix together the eggs and milk, and add to the squash mixture. Stir in the melted butter or margarine, and season with salt and pepper. Spread into a large baking dish, and top with the remaining cheese mixture. Bake for 25 minutes or until lightly browned.

MAKES 8 TO 10 SERVINGS

CALIFORNIA CASSEROLE

2 cups vegetable stock

¾ cup uncooked long grain rice

2 cups sour cream

2 4-ounce cans diced green chiles

½ cup chopped green onions

½ teaspoon salt

¼ teaspoon pepper

4 cups shredded Monterey Jack cheese

Preheat the oven to 350°. Lightly oil a 1½-quart casserole dish. In a saucepan bring the vegetable stock to a boil over medium heat. Add the rice. Reduce the heat to low and cook, stirring occasionally, for about 20 minutes, or until the liquid is absorbed. In a medium bowl mix together the sour cream, green chiles, green onions, salt, and pepper. Set aside. Spread half of the rice into the bottom of the casserole dish. Spread half of the sour cream mixture on top, followed by half of the Monterey Jack cheese. Continue layering, ending with cheese on top. Bake for 45 to 50 minutes or until the cheese is melted.

MAKES 6 SERVINGS

PEPPER CASSEROLE

1½ tablespoons olive oil

2   cups sliced onion

3   medium green bell peppers, thinly sliced

2   medium red bell peppers, thinly sliced

2   medium yellow bell peppers, thinly sliced

4   cloves garlic, minced

1   teaspoon salt

1½ teaspoons ground cumin

1   teaspoon dry mustard

2   tablespoons all-purpose flour

2   eggs

2   cups sour cream

2   cups sliced Monterey Jack cheese

Preheat the oven to 375°. Lightly oil an 8-inch square baking dish with olive oil. In a large skillet heat the remaining olive oil. Add the onion, and sauté for about 5 minutes over medium heat. Add the bell peppers, garlic, salt, cumin, and dry mustard. Sauté for another 8 to 10 minutes, then sprinkle in the flour. Cook and stir for about 5 minutes or until the peppers are very tender. Pour the mixture into the prepared baking dish. In a medium bowl beat together the eggs and sour cream with an electric mixer. Pour over the peppers, and top with Monterey Jack cheese slices. Bake for 45 minutes or until hot and bubbly.

MAKES 4 TO 6 SERVINGS

TWO-CHEESE POLENTA

1 cup yellow cornmeal

4 cups water

2 teaspoons salt

1 tablespoon butter or margarine

½ cup grated Parmesan cheese

1 teaspoon chopped fresh thyme

⅔ cup shredded Swiss cheese

Preheat the oven to 350°. Grease a 1½-quart casserole dish. In a 2-quart saucepan mix the cornmeal and ¾ cup water. Stir in 3¼ cups boiling water and the salt. Cook over medium-high heat, stirring constantly, until the mixture thickens and begins to boil. Reduce the heat, and stir in the butter or margarine, Parmesan cheese, and thyme. Cover and simmer for 10 minutes, stirring occasionally. Remove from the heat and stir until smooth. Spread half of the polenta into the prepared casserole dish. Top with ⅓ cup of the Swiss cheese. Repeat with the remaining polenta and Swiss cheese. Bake for 15 to 20 minutes or until hot and bubbly.

MAKES 4 TO 6 SERVINGS

TACO CASSEROLE

1 tablespoon vegetable oil
1 cup chopped onion
1 16-ounce jar chunky salsa
1 10-ounce can enchilada sauce
1 package (12) white corn taco shells,
 broken into pieces
1½ cups shredded Monterey Jack cheese
 Sour cream

Preheat the oven to 350°. In a large skillet heat the vegetable oil over medium-high heat. Add the onion and sauté for 1 to 2 minutes. Stir in the salsa and enchilada sauce. Reduce the heat and cook, stirring frequently, for about 5 minutes. Layer half of the taco shell pieces in an ungreased 9 x 13-inch baking dish. Top with half of the salsa mixture and half of the Monterey Jack cheese; repeat with another layer of taco shell pieces, salsa mixture, and cheese. Bake for 10 to 15 minutes or until the cheese is melted. Serve with sour cream.

MAKES 8 SERVINGS

LAYERED TAMALE PIE

1   15-ounce can kidney beans,
      undrained

1   large onion, chopped

4   cloves garlic, minced

2   medium green bell peppers, diced

2   medium carrots, diced

1   medium jalapeño pepper, seeded and
      diced

2   tablespoons oregano

1   tablespoon ground cumin

1   cup whole kernel corn

1   16-ounce can whole tomatoes,
      drained

3½ cups water

1½ cups yellow cornmeal

¼   teaspoon pepper

1   cup shredded Cheddar cheese

1   cup shredded Monterey Jack cheese

Preheat the oven to 350°. Drain the liquid from the kidney beans
into a large skillet. Bring the liquid to a boil over medium heat.
Add the onion, garlic, green peppers, carrots, jalapeño, oregano,
and cumin. Cover and cook, stirring occasionally, until the vegetables are tender and the liquid is absorbed. Add the kidney
beans, corn, and tomatoes, and cook uncovered, stirring occasionally, for about 15 minutes or until thickened. Set aside. In a

2-quart saucepan heat the water, cornmeal, and pepper to boiling, stirring constantly. Cook for 5 minutes or until well thickened. Pour half of the bean mixture into a 9-inch round baking dish, spreading evenly. Spread half of the cornmeal mixture over the beans, and sprinkle with half of the Cheddar cheese and half of the Monterey Jack cheese. Repeat the layers. Bake for 35 minutes or until bubbly and golden brown.

MAKES 6 SERVINGS

TORTILLA SKILLET

½   cup vegetable oil
12 corn tortillas, cut into ½-inch strips
8   medium green onions, chopped
1   16-ounce can whole tomatoes,
    drained
½   teaspoon oregano
½   teaspoon salt
⅛   teaspoon pepper
1   cup shredded Monterey Jack cheese
    Sour cream

In a large skillet heat the oil over medium heat. Cook the tortilla strips and green onions in the oil for about 10 minutes, stirring occasionally, until the tortillas are crisp. Stir in the tomatoes, oregano, salt, and pepper, and cook, stirring, for 2 to 3 minutes. Sprinkle with Monterey Jack cheese and heat just until the cheese is melted. Serve with sour cream.

MAKES 6 SERVINGS

MEXICAN JUMPING BEAN PIE

1	15-ounce can black beans, drained
1	15-ounce can pinto beans, drained
1	16-ounce can vegetarian refried beans
1	2-ounce can sliced black olives, drained
½	cup chopped green bell pepper
1	tablespoon ground cumin
1	tablespoon chili powder
5	8-inch flour tortillas
1½	cups shredded Monterey Jack cheese
	Salsa
	Sour cream

Preheat the oven to 350°. Lighly oil a 9-inch round baking dish. In a large saucepan heat the black beans, pinto beans, refried beans, olives, and bell pepper over medium-high heat. Season with the cumin and chili powder. Cook and stir until heated through, about 10 minutes. Lay one tortilla flat on the bottom of the prepared baking dish. Spread one-fourth of the bean mixture on the tortilla, and top with ¼ cup Monterey Jack cheese. Continue layering until the last tortilla is on top. Top with the remaining cheese. Bake for 20 minutes. Serve with salsa and sour cream.

MAKES 6 TO 8 SERVINGS

SOUTHERN RED BEANS AND RICE

14 ounces uncooked brown rice

2 15-ounce cans kidney beans, drained

1 24-ounce jar picante sauce

1½ tablespoons paprika

1 tablespoon chili powder

½ teaspoon crushed red pepper flakes

3 cups shredded sharp Cheddar cheese

Cook the rice according to the package directions. In a medium saucepan heat the beans, picante sauce, paprika, chili powder, and crushed red pepper flakes. Add the rice and simmer for about 15 minutes. Stir in the Cheddar cheese and let simmer for 5 to 10 more minutes.

MAKES 4 TO 6 SERVINGS

EASY VEGGIE CHILI

1	28-ounce can tomatoes, undrained
1	15-ounce can black beans, undrained
1	11-ounce can whole kernel corn, undrained
1	cup chunky salsa
1	cup chopped green bell pepper
1	cup chopped fresh mushrooms
1	cup chopped onions
¾	cup chopped celery
1	tablespoon chili powder
2	cups shredded Cheddar cheese

In a large saucepan heat the tomatoes, black beans, corn, salsa, bell pepper, mushrooms, onions, celery, and chili powder over medium-high heat. Bring to a boil, reduce the heat to low, and simmer for 10 minutes. Spoon the chili into serving bowls, and top with Cheddar cheese.

MAKES 8 SERVINGS

BEAN AND CHEESE CHIMICHANGAS WITH GUACAMOLE

2 16-ounce cans vegetarian refried beans
1 cup shredded Cheddar cheese
1 cup shredded Monterey Jack cheese
⅔ cup chunky salsa
2 teaspoons ground cumin
¼ cup vegetable oil
8 large flour tortillas

Guacamole:
1 large avocado
2 teaspoons lime juice
¼ teaspoon minced garlic
½ teaspoon salt
3 teaspoons salsa

Sour cream
Salsa

Preheat the oven to 475°. Lightly oil a 9 x 13-inch baking dish. In a large bowl combine the beans, Cheddar cheese, Monterey Jack cheese, ⅔ cup salsa, and cumin. Mix well. In a large skillet heat the vegetable oil over medium heat. Spoon about ½ cup of the bean mixture into the center of a tortilla. Fold up both sides of the tortilla, followed by the top and bottom, and place, seam side down, in the skillet. Fry each side until golden brown, and place in the prepared baking dish. Continue with the remaining tortillas. Bake for 10 minutes.

Cut the avocado in half and scoop out the pulp into a medium bowl. Mash with a fork. Add the lime juice, garlic, salt, and 3 teaspoons salsa, and mix well. Serve the chimichangas with guacamole, sour cream, and salsa.

MAKES 8 SERVINGS

STACKED ENCHILADAS VERDE

1 28-ounce can green enchilada sauce
1 4-ounce can diced green chiles, drained
18 corn tortillas
1½ cups shredded mild Cheddar cheese
1½ cups shredded Monterey Jack cheese
1 medium onion, diced
1 2-ounce can sliced black olives, drained

Preheat the oven to 350°. Lightly oil a 9 x 13-inch baking dish. In a large saucepan mix the enchilada sauce and green chiles over low heat. Pass 6 of the corn tortillas through the enchilada sauce, and place them side by side in the prepared baking dish. Top with one-third of the Cheddar and Monterey Jack cheese, one-third of the onion, and about ½ cup enchilada sauce. Add two more layers of corn tortillas topped with cheese, onion, and sauce. Top with the remaining sauce and olives, and bake for 45 to 50 minutes or until the cheese is thoroughly melted.

MAKES 6 TO 8 SERVINGS

PINEAPPLE ENCHILADAS

1	20-ounce can crushed pineapple, drained
¼	cup sour cream
2	cups shredded Cheddar cheese
1	10-ounce can enchilada sauce
6	8-inch flour tortillas

Preheat the oven to 375°. In a medium bowl combine the pineapple, sour cream, and 1 cup Cheddar cheese. Pour ¼ cup enchilada sauce into a large casserole dish. Place one-sixth of the pineapple mixture in a line down the center of each flour tortilla. Roll the tortillas and place them in the casserole dish, seam side down. Pour the remaining enchilada sauce over the tortilla rolls and top with the remaining cheese. Bake, covered, for 30 minutes.

MAKES 4 TO 6 SERVINGS

SPINACH ENCHILADAS

½   cup vegetable oil
½   cup chopped onion
1   clove garlic, minced
3   cups chopped fresh spinach
2   cups sliced fresh mushrooms
2   10-ounce cans enchilada sauce
12 corn tortillas
1½ cups shredded Monterey Jack cheese
    Sour cream

Preheat the oven to 350°. In a large saucepan heat 1 tablespoon of
the vegetable oil over medium-high heat. Sauté the onion and
garlic for 3 to 4 minutes. Add the spinach and mushrooms and
cook, stirring occasionally, for 2 to 3 minutes or until the spinach
is cooked through. Stir in ½ cup of the enchilada sauce and mix
well. Reduce the heat. Pour the remaining enchilada sauce in a
small skillet over low heat. In a separate skillet heat the remaining
vegetable oil over medium-low heat. Soak the tortillas in the vegetable oil for approximately 30 seconds or until soft; drain on
paper towels. Soak the tortillas in the enchilada sauce for approximately 30 seconds and place in a large baking dish. Arrange ¼
cup of the spinach mixture and 1 tablespoon Monterey Jack
cheese in a line down the center of each tortilla, and roll the tortilla, placing seam side down in the baking dish. Top the enchi-
ladas with the remaining enchilada sauce and cheese. Bake for 10
to 12 minutes. Let cool; serve with sour cream.

MAKES 6 SERVINGS

BEAN TOSTADAS

2	16-ounce cans vegetarian refried beans
1	16-ounce jar chunky salsa
1	medium onion, chopped
1	tablespoon chili powder
16	flat corn tostada shells
1½	cups sour cream
1	head iceberg lettuce, rinsed and shredded
1	cup shredded mild Cheddar cheese
1	cup shredded Monterey Jack cheese
3	medium tomatoes, chopped
1	8-ounce can sliced olives, drained

In a medium saucepan mix the refried beans, half of the salsa, the onion, and the chili powder over medium heat. Cook, stirring occasionally, until heated through. Place the tostada shells on a baking sheet and warm in the oven for about 5 minutes. Top each tostada shell with ¼ cup of the bean mixture, followed by 2 tablespoons sour cream and 1 tablespoon salsa. Top with lettuce, Cheddar cheese, Monterey Jack cheese, tomatoes, and olives. Serve immediately.

MAKES 8 SERVINGS

BEAN AND FETA QUESADILLAS

2 15-ounce cans pinto beans, drained
1½ cups feta cheese
1 cup chopped onion
1 cup chopped fresh parsley
2 teaspoons chili powder
1 teaspoon ground cumin
6 large flour tortillas
1 teaspoon vegetable oil
  Salsa
  Sour cream

In a blender combine the beans, feta cheese, onion, parsley, chili powder, and cumin, processing until a chunky purée forms. Spoon one-sixth of the mixture onto a tortilla, spreading the mixture evenly over half of the tortilla. Fold the tortilla over and brush the top lightly with vegetable oil. Repeat with the remaining tortillas. In a large skillet heat about 1 teaspoon vegetable oil over medium-high heat. Fry each quesadilla in the skillet until the beans are heated through and the tortilla is golden brown, turning once. Serve with salsa and sour cream.

MAKES 6 SERVINGS

QUICK CHILE RELLENOS

3 4-ounce cans whole green chiles,
   drained
9 8-inch flour tortillas
3 cups shredded Pepper Jack cheese
1 19-ounce can enchilada sauce
1 cup sour cream
¼ cup chopped fresh cilantro

Preheat the oven to 350°. Grease a 9 x 13-inch baking dish. Split
each chile lengthwise into halves and remove the seeds. Arrange 2
chile halves near the outer edge of each tortilla, and top with
about ¼ cup Pepper Jack cheese. Roll the tortilla, enchilada-style,
to enclose the chiles and cheese. Repeat the process with the
remaining tortillas, chiles, and cheese. Arrange the filled tortillas
seam side down in the prepared baking dish. In a small bowl
whisk together the enchilada sauce and sour cream. Spoon over
the filled tortillas. Bake for 30 minutes or until bubbly. Top with
cilantro.

MAKES 6 SERVINGS

FETTUCCINE ALFREDO

24 ounces fettuccine pasta
½ cup butter or margarine
2 cups whipping cream
1½ cups grated Parmesan cheese
1 teaspoon salt
1 teaspoon pepper

Cook the pasta according to the package directions and drain. In a large saucepan heat the butter or margarine and 1½ cups cream. Simmer over medium heat for about 1 minute. Reduce the heat to low, add the pasta, and mix well. Add the Parmesan cheese, the remainder of the cream, the salt, and pepper. Stir until the cream has thickened and serve immediately.

MAKES 6 SERVINGS

FETTUCCINE WITH SALSA CRUDA AND FETA

16 ounces fettuccine pasta
5 medium tomatoes, chopped
½ small red onion, chopped
1 cup chopped fresh basil
½ cup pitted chopped kalamata olives
2 tablespoons olive oil
1 cup crumbled feta cheese

Cook the pasta according to the package directions and drain. In a medium bowl combine the tomatoes, onion, basil, and olives. Toss the fettuccine with the olive oil. Serve the pasta topped with the tomato mixture and feta cheese.

MAKES 6 TO 8 SERVINGS

ARTICHOKE SPINACH LASAGNE

9   uncooked lasagne noodles
1½ tablespoons vegetable oil
1   onion, chopped
4   cloves garlic, chopped
1   15-ounce can vegetable stock
1   tablespoon chopped fresh rosemary
2   6-ounce jars artichoke hearts,
     drained and chopped
1   10-ounce package frozen chopped
     spinach, thawed
1   26-ounce jar marinara sauce
3   cups shredded mozzarella cheese
1   4-ounce package herb and garlic feta cheese

Preheat the oven to 350°. Oil a 9 x 13-inch baking dish. Cook the
noodles according to the package directions and drain. In a large
skillet heat 1 tablespoon vegetable oil and sauté the onion and
garlic for about 3 minutes. Stir in the vegetable stock and rosemary, and bring to a boil. Add the artichoke hearts and spinach.
Reduce the heat, cover, and simmer for 5 minutes, stirring occasionally. Stir in the marinara sauce. Spread one-third of the artichoke mixture in the bottom of the prepared baking dish, and top
with 3 cooked noodles. Sprinkle 1 cup mozzarella cheese over the
noodles. Repeat the layers 2 more times, and top with feta cheese.
Bake, covered, for 40 minutes. Uncover and bake for 15 more
minutes or until hot and bubbly.

MAKES 6 TO 8 SERVINGS

DOUBLE CHEESE DISH

12   ounces egg noodles
1   tablespoon olive oil
1   large onion, diced
1   15-ounce can tomato sauce
4   ounces cream cheese
3   cups cottage cheese
2   cups sour cream

Preheat the oven to 350°. Cook the egg noodles according to the package directions and drain. In a large skillet heat the olive oil and sauté the onion until tender. Add the tomato sauce and let simmer for 1 minute. Add the cream cheese and cottage cheese, stirring together until well blended. Stir in the egg noodles and sour cream until all ingredients are mixed thoroughly. Pour into a 2-quart casserole dish, and bake for 30 minutes.

MAKES 6 SERVINGS

ARTICHOKE GARLIC PASTA

14 ounces seashell pasta

2 tablespoons butter or margarine

⅛ teaspoon minced garlic

1 tablespoon all-purpose flour

¾ cup whipping cream

⅓ cup grated Parmesan cheese

¼ cup parsley flakes

Salt and pepper to taste

1 6-ounce jar quartered artichoke hearts, drained

Cook the pasta according to the package directions and drain. In a saucepan melt the butter or margarine and sauté the garlic for about 1 minute. Stir in the flour, blending until smooth. Add the cream, stirring constantly, until thickened. Stir in the Parmesan cheese, parsley flakes, salt, and pepper; continue stirring until the cheese is melted and the mixture is well blended. Add the pasta and artichokes, and cook until thoroughly heated.

MAKES 6 TO 8 SERVINGS

MACARONI AND CHEESE

 6 ounces elbow macaroni
 3 tablespoons butter or margarine
 ¼ cup finely chopped onion
 2 tablespoons all-purpose flour
 ½ teaspoon salt
   Pepper to taste
 2 cups milk
 2 cups American cheese, cubed

Preheat the oven to 350°. Cook the macaroni according to the package directions and drain. In a saucepan melt the butter or margarine and sauté the onion until tender. Add the flour, salt, and pepper, stirring until smooth. Add the milk, stirring constantly, until thickened. Stir in the American cheese and cook, stirring, until the cheese is melted. Add the macaroni and mix well. Pour the mixture into a 1½-quart casserole dish, and bake for 30 to 35 minutes.

MAKES 6 SERVINGS

PASTA AND BROCCOLI WITH GORGONZOLA SAUCE

16	ounces corkscrew pasta
3	cups broccoli florets
1	cup whipping cream
8	ounces Gorgonzola cheese, rind removed
½	cup butter or margarine, softened
¼	cup grated Parmesan cheese
⅓	cup finely chopped fresh parsley

Cook the pasta according to the package directions and drain. Boil the broccoli in 2 cups of water for 2 to 4 minutes, and rinse with cold water. In a medium saucepan heat the cream and simmer for 5 minutes. Stir in the Gorgonzola cheese and ¼ cup butter or margarine. Cook over medium-low heat, stirring, until the sauce is smooth. Toss the pasta with the broccoli and the remaining butter or margarine. Add the Parmesan cheese and parsley and mix thoroughly. Toss with the Gorgonzola cheese sauce before serving.

MAKES 6 SERVINGS

SPINACH AND FETA PASTA

8   ounces penne pasta
2   tablespoons olive oil
½   cup chopped onion
1   clove garlic, minced
3   cups chopped tomatoes
1   cup sliced fresh mushrooms
2   cups chopped fresh spinach
1   pinch red pepper flakes
2   cups feta cheese

Cook the pasta according to the package directions and drain. In a large skillet heat the olive oil over medium-high heat. Add the onion and garlic, and cook until golden brown. Mix in the tomatoes, mushrooms, spinach, and red pepper flakes, and cook until the spinach and tomatoes are thoroughly heated. Reduce the heat to medium, stir in the pasta and feta cheese, and cook just until the cheese is melted.

MAKES 4 TO 6 SERVINGS

SPINACH PASTA SUPREME

8 ounces seashell pasta

1 10-ounce package frozen chopped spinach, thawed and drained

2 cups cottage cheese

½ cup dry breadcrumbs

3 tablespoons butter or margarine, melted

Preheat the oven to 425°. Cook the pasta according to the package directions and drain. In a small casserole dish combine the cooked pasta, spinach, and cottage cheese, and mix well. In a small bowl mix together the breadcrumbs and butter or margarine, and sprinkle over the spinach mixture. Bake for 15 minutes or until heated through.

MAKES 4 TO 6 SERVINGS

STUFFED SHELLS

24 jumbo pasta shells
2   cups spaghetti sauce
2   cups ricotta cheese
1   cup shredded mozzarella cheese
½   cup grated Parmesan cheese
2   tablespoons chopped fresh parsley
½   teaspoon pepper

Preheat the oven to 350°. Cook the pasta shells until just tender and drain. Spread half of the spaghetti sauce into a 9 x 13-inch ungreased casserole dish, and arrange the pasta shells on top. In a medium bowl mix together the ricotta cheese, mozzarella cheese, Parmesan cheese, parsley, and pepper. Spoon about 2 tablespoons of the cheese mixture into each shell, and top with the remaining spaghetti sauce. Bake for about 45 minutes.

MAKES 8 TO 12 SERVINGS

BAKED ZITI

16 ounces ziti pasta

2 tablespoons vegetable oil

1 medium onion, chopped

1 26-ounce jar marinara sauce

6 ounces Provolone cheese, sliced

1½ cups sour cream

1½ cups shredded mozzarella cheese

2 tablespoons grated Parmesan cheese

Preheat the oven to 350°. Lightly oil a large baking dish. Cook the pasta according to the package directions and drain. In a large skillet heat the vegetable oil and brown the onion. Add the marinara sauce and simmer for about 15 minutes. Spread half of the ziti pasta in the prepared baking dish. Top with the Provolone cheese slices, sour cream, and half of the marinara sauce mixture. Add the remaining ziti, followed by the mozzarella cheese and the remaining sauce. Sprinkle with Parmesan cheese. Bake for 30 minutes or until the cheeses are melted.

MAKES 8 SERVINGS

DOUBLE BUBBLE PIZZA

2   12-ounce packages refrigerated
    biscuit dough
1   14-ounce can pizza sauce
1½ cups shredded mozzarella cheese
1   medium onion, chopped
1   2-ounce can sliced black olives
1   cup sliced fresh mushrooms
1   green bell pepper, chopped
1   clove garlic, minced
1   cup shredded Cheddar cheese

Preheat the oven to 400°. Generously oil a 9 x 13-inch baking dish. Place the uncooked biscuits side-by-side in the bottom of the prepared baking dish. Using a spoon, evenly press down on the dough slightly to firm. Spread the pizza sauce evenly over the biscuit dough, and sprinkle with half of the mozzarella cheese. Evenly sprinkle onion, olives, mushrooms, bell pepper, and garlic over the pizza. Bake for 20 to 25 minutes. Top with the remaining mozzarella cheese and the Cheddar cheese, and bake an additional 5 to 10 minutes, until the cheese is melted.

MAKES 8 SERVINGS

SUN-DRIED TOMATO CALZONES

2 cups shredded mozzarella cheese
1½ cups chopped goat cheese
½ cup chopped sun-dried tomatoes
2 pounds bread dough

Preheat the oven to 450°. Grease a large baking sheet. In a medium bowl combine the mozzarella cheese, goat cheese, and sun-dried tomatoes, and mix well. Divide the dough into 6 pieces. On a floured surface, roll each piece of dough into a 7-inch round. Top the left half of each round with one-sixth of the cheese mixture, about ⅔ cup, spreading evenly. Moisten the edges of the dough with water, and fold the right side over so that the edges meet. Press the edges to seal, then crimp the edges and cut three ½-inch slits in top. Place the calzones on the prepared baking sheet and bake for 20 to 25 minutes or until well browned.

MAKES 6 SERVINGS

THREE-CHEESE SQUARES

½ cup olive oil
1 cup ricotta cheese
2 cups feta cheese
3 ounces cream cheese, softened
2 tablespoons all-purpose flour
2 eggs
½ teaspoon nutmeg
¼ teaspoon pepper
½ cup chopped fresh parsley
12 sheets 16 x 24-inch phyllo dough,
    thawed and cut into fourths

Preheat the oven to 375°. With a pastry brush coat the bottom of a 9 x 13-inch baking dish with olive oil. Beat together the ricotta cheese, feta cheese, cream cheese, flour, eggs, nutmeg, and pepper with an electric mixer until well blended. Stir in the parsley. Line the prepared baking dish with one ¼-sheet of phyllo dough. Lightly brush the dough in the baking dish with olive oil. Place another sheet in the baking dish, and brush with olive oil. Continue with half of the phyllo dough. Spread the cheese mixture evenly over the phyllo dough. Repeat the phyllo and olive oil layers with the remaining phyllo dough. Bake for 35 minutes or until the top of the pastry is golden and crisp.

MAKES 8 TO 10 SERVINGS

SIDE DISHES

GARLIC-CHEESE ASPARAGUS

1   pound fresh asparagus, trimmed
2   cups Italian-seasoned dry breadcrumbs
¼   teaspoon salt
¼   teaspoon pepper
1   teaspoon garlic powder
½   cup grated Parmesan cheese
4   tablespoons butter or margarine, sliced

Preheat the oven to 400°. Place the asparagus in a 9 x 13-inch baking dish, and cover with breadcrumbs, salt, pepper, garlic powder, and Parmesan cheese. Lay the butter or margarine slices on top. Bake, covered, for 30 minutes. Remove the cover, and bake for 5 more minutes or until browned.

MAKES 4 TO 6 SERVINGS

ASPARAGUS MILANO

2 cups marinara sauce
1½ pounds fresh asparagus, trimmed
1 cup shredded mozzarella cheese

Preheat the oven to 350°. Grease a 9 x 13-inch baking dish.
Spread 1 cup marinara sauce over the bottom of the dish. Place
the asparagus on top of the sauce, and top with the remaining
marinara sauce. Sprinkle the mozzarella cheese over top. Bake 40
to 45 minutes or until the asparagus is tender.

MAKES 6 SERVINGS

EASY CHEESY ASPARAGUS

2   15-ounce cans asparagus, drained
1   10-ounce can condensed cheese
    soup
8   cherry tomatoes, cut in half
2   tablespoons chopped green onion

Preheat the oven to 350°. Arrange the asparagus spears in a
9-inch round baking dish. Spoon the cheese soup evenly over the
the spears. Bake for 10 minutes or until hot. Garnish with tomato
halves and green onion, and bake for an additional 3 to 5 minutes.

MAKES 6 TO 8 SERVINGS

MEDITERRANEAN POTATOES AND ARTICHOKES

8   small red potatoes, cut into fourths
2   teaspoons olive oil
1   small onion, cut into wedges
4   cloves garlic, finely chopped
2   6-ounce jars quartered artichoke
    hearts, drained
2   plum tomatoes, chopped
12 small pimiento-stuffed olives
2   tablespoons pesto
2   tablespoons chopped fresh parsley
⅓   cup feta cheese

Boil the potatoes for 15 minutes or until almost tender and drain. In a large skillet heat the olive oil over medium-high heat. Add the onion and garlic and sauté for 2 minutes. Add the potatoes, and cook for about 5 minutes, stirring, until tender. Add the artichokes, tomatoes, olives, and pesto. Cook, stirring occasionally, until hot. Sprinkle with parsley and feta cheese.

MAKES 6 SERVINGS

ARTICHOKE HEARTS AU GRATIN

4   6-ounce jars quartered artichoke hearts, undrained
¼   cup butter or margarine
¾   teaspoon salt
1   teaspoon onion salt
¼   teaspoon pepper
¼   teaspoon dry mustard
⅓   cup all-purpose flour
1½ cups milk
1   cup grated Swiss cheese
2   tablespoons dry breadcrumbs
½   teaspoon paprika

Preheat the oven to 450°. Drain the artichoke hearts and reserve ½ cup liquid. Arrange the artichoke hearts in a single layer in a shallow baking dish. In a medium saucepan melt the butter or margarine. Stir in the salt, onion salt, pepper, dry mustard, and flour. Gradually stir in the artichoke liquid and milk, stirring constantly, until thickened. Remove from the heat. Stir in ½ cup Swiss cheese, blending well. Pour over the artichokes. Sprinkle with the remaining cheese, breadcrumbs, and paprika. Bake for 15 minutes.

MAKES 8 SERVINGS

MUSTARD BEANS

⅓ cup butter or margarine
2   tablespoons all-purpose flour
1   cup milk
2   teaspoons mustard
4   ounces American cheese, cubed
    Salt and pepper to taste
2   15-ounce cans yellow wax beans,
    drained
½   cup dry breadcrumbs

Preheat the oven to 350°. In a medium saucepan melt 2 table-spoons butter or margarine over medium heat. Reduce the heat to low, and gradually stir in the flour to form a thick paste. Slowly blend in the milk, stirring constantly, and bring to a low boil. Reduce the heat, and stir in the mustard, American cheese, salt, and pepper. Continue stirring until the cheese is completely melted. Place one-half of the beans in a medium baking dish. Layer with one-half of the American cheese mixture. Top with the remaining beans and cheese mixture. In a small saucepan melt the remaining butter or margarine, and mix in the breadcrumbs. Sprinkle the breadcrumb mixture over the cheese layer, and bake for 30 minutes or until lightly brown.

MAKES 6 TO 8 SERVINGS

BRILLIANT BROCCOLI

1   16-ounce package frozen chopped
    broccoli
1   tablespoon milk
½   cup grated Cheddar cheese
½   cup mayonnaise
½   teaspoon oregano

Cook the broccoli according to the package directions and drain.
In a small saucepan mix together the milk, Cheddar cheese, mayonnaise, and oregano, and cook over low heat, stirring frequently,
until the cheese is melted and the ingredients are thoroughly
mixed. Pour over the broccoli and toss to coat.

MAKES 6 SERVINGS

BRUSSELS SPROUTS BAKE

2   10-ounce packages frozen Brussels sprouts

2   tablespoons butter or margarine, melted

1   10-ounce can condensed cream of mushroom soup

1   egg, beaten

1   cup Cheddar cheese, shredded

⅔   cup dry breadcrumbs

Preheat the oven to 350°. In a medium saucepan boil the frozen Brussels sprouts for 6 to 8 minutes or until tender; drain. In a medium bowl mix together the butter or margarine, soup, egg, Cheddar cheese, and ⅓ cup breadcrumbs. Add the Brussels sprouts and mix well. Transfer to a medium baking dish, and sprinkle with the remaining breadcrumbs. Cover, and bake for 25 minutes. Uncover, and bake for 5 more minutes or until lightly browned and bubbly.

MAKES 8 TO 10 SERVINGS

SCALLOPED CABBAGE

1   medium head cabbage, cut into
    small wedges
2   tablespoons butter or margarine
2   tablespoons all-purpose flour
½   teaspoon salt
1   cup milk
⅔   cup shredded American cheese
½   cup crushed butter crackers

Preheat the oven to 350°. Lightly oil a 2-quart baking dish. Boil the cabbage for about 10 minutes or until just tender; drain. In a small saucepan melt the butter or margarine over low heat. Blend in the flour and salt, stirring, until smooth. Gradually add the milk, stirring constantly, until slightly thickened. Stir in the American cheese and mix well. Transfer the cabbage to the prepared baking dish and stir in the cheese sauce. Sprinkle the cracker crumbs on top. Bake for 25 to 30 minutes.

MAKES 6 SERVINGS

CARROTS AU GRATIN

4½ cups sliced carrots

⅔ cup crushed butter crackers

3 tablespoons butter or margarine, melted

½ cup chopped onion

3 tablespoons all-purpose flour

½ teaspoon salt

¼ teaspoon pepper

1½ cups milk

⅔ cup shredded American cheese

Preheat the oven to 350°. Place the carrots in a steamer over 1 inch of boiling water, and cover. Steam for 7 to 8 minutes, or until just tender. Drain. In a small bowl combine the crushed crackers with 1 tablespoon butter or margarine. Mix well and set aside. In a medium skillet heat the remaining 2 tablespoons of butter or margarine over low heat, and sauté the onion until tender. Stir in the flour, salt, and pepper. Gradually add the milk, stirring constantly. Increase the heat to medium and cook until thickened. Add the American cheese and stir until smooth. Fold in the carrots. Pour the mixture into a 9 x 13-inch baking dish and top with the cracker crumb mixture. Bake for 20 minutes or until bubbly.

MAKES 8 SERVINGS

CHEESE-FROSTED CAULIFLOWER

1 pound cauliflower florets
½ cup mayonnaise
1½ teaspoons mustard
1 cup shredded American cheese

Preheat the oven to 375°. In a large saucepan boil the cauliflower florets until tender. Place the cauliflower florets in an 8-inch square baking dish. Stir together the mayonnaise and mustard, and spread over the cauliflower. Top with the American cheese. Bake for about 5 minutes or until the cheese begins to melt.

MAKES 6 SERVINGS

SAUCY CELERY

6 tablespoons butter or margarine
4 cups thinly sliced celery
1 cup chopped fresh mushrooms
3 tablespoons all-purpose flour
1 teaspoon salt
1 cup milk
2 tablespoons chopped green bell
  pepper
1 2-ounce jar chopped pimientos
1 cup shredded Cheddar cheese
1 cup dry breadcrumbs

Preheat the oven to 350°. In a small saucepan melt 2 tablespoons of the butter or margarine over medium heat, and sauté the celery and mushrooms until tender, about 5 minutes. In a large saucepan melt 2 tablespoons butter or margarine. Stir in the flour and salt. Slowly add the milk, stirring constantly, until the mixture is smooth and creamy. Add the celery mixture, bell pepper, and pimientos, and mix well. Stir in the Cheddar cheese, and cook, stirring, until melted. In a small bowl blend the breadcrumbs and the remaining butter or margarine. Transfer the celery mixture to a medium baking dish, and sprinkle with the breadcrumb mixture. Bake for 20 minutes or until lightly browned.

MAKES 8 SERVINGS

BAKED CORN

¼ cup butter or margarine, softened

12 ounces cream cheese, softened

1 11-ounce can whole kernel corn, drained

1 15-ounce can cream-style corn

1 4-ounce can diced green chiles

½ cup chopped fresh onion

1 6-ounce can French-fried onions

Preheat the oven to 350°. In a medium bowl beat together the butter or margarine and cream cheese with an electric mixer. Stir in the whole kernel corn, cream-style corn, green chiles, fresh onion, and half of the French-fried onions. Pour the mixture into a 1-quart casserole dish. Bake for 15 minutes. Sprinkle the remaining French-fried onions over the top of the casserole, and bake for an additional 15 minutes.

MAKES 8 SERVINGS

CORN AND ZUCCHINI MEDLEY

1 tablespoon vegetable oil
2 cups chopped zucchini
1½ cups fresh corn kernels
1 small onion, chopped
    Pepper to taste
¼ cup shredded Monterey Jack cheese

In a large skillet heat the vegetable oil over medium heat. Sauté the zucchini, corn, and onion until just tender, about 10 minutes. Season with pepper. Spoon the vegetables into a bowl, and sprinkle with Monterey Jack cheese.

MAKES 6 SERVINGS

BLUE GREEN BEANS

1   pound fresh green beans, cut into
    2-inch pieces
¼   cup vegetable oil
½   cup chopped walnuts, toasted
1   cup crumbled blue cheese

In a saucepan with one inch of water in the bottom bring the green beans to a boil over medium-high heat, and cook for 5 minutes or until just tender. Remove from the heat, drain, and set aside. In a large skillet heat the vegetable oil over medium heat. Add the green beans and cook for 2 to 3 minutes. Sprinkle with walnuts and crumbled blue cheese, and toss to coat.

MAKES 6 SERVINGS

CREAMY FRENCH GREEN BEANS

1   8-ounce round Brie cheese, rind removed

2   tablespoons butter or margarine

1½ pounds fresh green beans, trimmed

10 ounces baby portabella (Cremini) mushrooms, sliced

⅓   cup whipping cream

½   teaspoon salt

¼   teaspoon pepper

3   tablespoons chopped walnuts, toasted

Cut the Brie cheese round into ½-inch cubes. In a large skillet melt the butter or margarine over medium-high heat. Add the green beans and cook, stirring occasionally, for 6 to 7 minutes. Add the sliced mushrooms. Cook for 5 minutes or until the green beans are just tender. Stir in the cream, salt, and pepper. Remove the skillet from the heat, and stir in the Brie cheese until melted. Top with toasted walnuts.

MAKES 8 SERVINGS

GARLIC GREEN BEANS

1   tablespoon butter or margarine
3   tablespoons olive oil
1   medium head garlic, peeled and
     sliced
2   14-ounce cans green beans, drained
     Salt and pepper to taste
¼   cup grated Parmesan cheese

In a large skillet heat the butter or margarine and olive oil over
medium heat. Add the garlic, and cook until lightly browned, stirring frequently. Stir in the green beans, and season with salt and
pepper. Cook until the green beans are tender, about 10 minutes.
Remove from the heat, and sprinkle with Parmesan cheese.

MAKES 6 SERVINGS

CREAMY PARMESAN LEEKS

3   leeks, thinly sliced
¼   cup water
1½ tablespoons butter or margarine
¾   cup whipping cream
½   cup grated Parmesan cheese
    Pepper to taste

In a medium saucepan combine the leeks, water, and butter or margarine. Bring to a boil. Reduce the heat to low, cover, and simmer for 15 minutes, stirring occasionally. Gradually stir in the cream, mixing well, until thoroughly heated. Remove from the heat, and fold in the Parmesan cheese. Season with pepper.

MAKES 6 SERVINGS

BAKED ONIONS

6 medium onions, sliced
¼ cup butter or margarine
2 cloves garlic, finely chopped
¼ cup vegetable stock
¼ cup grated Parmesan cheese
2 tablespoons chopped fresh parsley

Preheat the oven to 350°. Place the onions in a medium baking dish. Pour water into the dish to ¼-inch depth. Cover and bake for about 35 to 40 minutes or until tender.

In a medium saucepan heat the butter or margarine over medium-high heat. Sauté the garlic until golden brown. Stir in the vegetable stock, Parmesan cheese, and parsley. Pour over the onions.

MAKES 6 SERVINGS

BAKED PINEAPPLE

1   20-ounce can pineapple chunks,
    undrained
3   tablespoons sugar
6   tablespoons butter or margarine,
    melted
3   tablespoons all-purpose flour
1¼ cups shredded Cheddar cheese
1   cup crushed butter crackers

Preheat the oven to 350°. Lightly butter a 1½-quart baking dish.
Drain the pineapple chunks, reserving 3 tablespoons juice. In a
medium bowl combine the pineapple, reserved juice, sugar, butter
or margarine, flour, and Cheddar cheese. Mix well. Spoon the
mixture into the prepared baking dish and top with cracker
crumbs. Bake for 30 minutes or until bubbly.

MAKES 6 SERVINGS

CHEESY CREAMED SPINACH

2   10-ounce packages frozen chopped spinach
1   10-ounce package dry onion soup mix
2   cups sour cream
½   cup shredded Cheddar cheese

Preheat the oven to 350°. Oil a 2-quart baking dish. Cook the spinach according to the package directions and drain. In a medium bowl combine the spinach, soup mix, and sour cream. Spoon into the prepared baking dish and top with Cheddar cheese. Bake for about 25 minutes or until heated through.

MAKES 8 TO 10 SERVINGS

SPINACH MADELEINE

2   10-ounce packages frozen chopped spinach

4   tablespoons butter or margarine

2   tablespoons all-purpose flour

2   tablespoons chopped onions

½   cup condensed milk

½   teaspoon garlic salt

½   teaspoon pepper

1   teaspoon Worcestershire sauce

1½ cups shredded Pepper Jack cheese

½   cup dry breadcrumbs

Preheat the oven to 350°. Cook the spinach according to the package directions and drain, reserving ½ cup liquid. In a medium saucepan melt the butter or margarine over low heat. Whisk in the flour until smooth. Add the onions and cook until soft. Slowly add the milk and reserved spinach liquid, stirring constantly, until the sauce is smooth. Add the garlic salt, pepper, Worcestershire sauce, and Pepper Jack cheese, stirring until well blended. Combine with the spinach. Pour into a 1½-quart baking dish and top with the breadcrumbs. Bake for 15 to 20 minutes or until bubbly.

MAKES 6 SERVINGS

NUTTY SWISS CHARD

2 tablespoons peanut oil

2 medium shallots, chopped

2 bunches Swiss chard, cut into 2-inch pieces

¼ cup feta cheese, crumbled

2 tablespoons toasted pine nuts

Salt and pepper to taste

In a large skillet or wok heat the oil over medium heat. Add the shallots, and sauté for 1 minute or until the shallots begin to brown. Mix in the Swiss chard. Reduce the heat, cover, and cook for 2 to 3 minutes, stirring occasionally. Remove from the heat and stir in the feta cheese. Mix in the pine nuts and season with salt and pepper.

MAKES 4 SERVINGS

TOMATOES OREGANO

⅛ cup grated Romano cheese
½ cup dry breadcrumbs
1 clove garlic, minced
¼ cup chopped fresh parsley
Salt and pepper to taste
½ teaspoon oregano
4 large tomatoes, sliced ¼-inch thick
1 tablespoon olive oil

Preheat the oven to 400°. In a medium bowl mix together the Romano cheese, breadcrumbs, garlic, parsley, salt, pepper, and oregano. Place the tomato slices close together on a large baking sheet. Sprinkle with the cheese mixture. Drizzle with olive oil. Bake for 40 minutes.

MAKES 4 TO 6 SERVINGS

PEPPER MUSHROOM SKILLET

½   cup vegetable stock
2   teaspoons butter or margarine
1   large red bell pepper, cut into 1-inch
    squares
1   yellow bell pepper, cut into 1-inch
    squares
2   green bell peppers, cut into 1-inch
    squares
3   cups sliced fresh mushrooms
1   teaspoon tarragon
    Salt and pepper to taste
2   tablespoons grated Parmesan cheese

In a large skillet heat the vegetable stock and butter or margarine
over medium heat. Sauté the bell peppers and mushrooms for 7 to
8 minutes, or until the mushrooms are tender. Stir in the tarragon
and season with salt and pepper. Sprinkle with Parmesan cheese.

MAKES 8 SERVINGS

ZUCCHINI BOATS

6	medium zucchini
4	cups water
2	cups dry breadcrumbs
2	eggs, lightly beaten
1	large tomato, diced
⅓	cup grated Romano cheese
¼	cup finely chopped fresh parsley
2	cloves garlic, minced
½	cup vegetable stock
½	teaspoon salt
⅛	teaspoon pepper
2	tablespoons butter or margarine, melted

Preheat the oven to 350°. Lightly grease a large baking sheet. Cut the zucchini in half lengthwise. Scoop out and reserve the pulp, leaving a ⅜-inch shell. In a saucepan boil the shells in water for 2 minutes; drain and place on the prepared baking sheet. Chop the zucchini pulp and place in a bowl. Add the breadcrumbs, eggs, tomato, Romano cheese, parsley, and garlic. Stir in the vegetable stock, salt, and pepper. Spoon the mixture into the zucchini shells and drizzle with butter or margarine. Bake for 20 minutes or until golden brown.

MAKES 6 SERVINGS

ZUCCHINI PARMESAN

4   medium zucchini
1   medium onion, sliced
1   tablespoon olive oil
    Garlic salt to taste
½   teaspoon oregano
⅛   teaspoon red pepper flakes
1   8-ounce can tomato sauce
¼   cup grated Parmesan cheese
8   ounces Provolone cheese, sliced

Cut the zucchini in half lengthwise. In a large skillet heat the olive oil and cook the onion until tender. Add the zucchini halves, cut side up. Sprinkle with garlic salt, oregano, and red pepper flakes. Top with tomato sauce. Cover and cook until just tender, about 10 minutes. Sprinkle with Parmesan cheese, top with the Provolone slices, and cover. Cook until the cheese begins to melt. Serve immediately.

MAKES 4 TO 6 SERVINGS

VEGETABLE GRATIN

2	tablespoons olive oil
¼	cup chopped onions
2	red bell peppers, sliced
2	medium zucchini, sliced
2	medium turnips, sliced
	Salt and pepper to taste
2	tomatoes, chopped
4	tablespoons grated Parmesan cheese

In a large saucepan heat the olive oil, and add the onions and red bell peppers. Cook, stirring, for about 1 minute. Add the zucchini, turnips, salt, and pepper. Cook, stirring frequently, for about 5 minutes. Add the tomatoes, and bring to boil. Reduce the heat, cover tightly, and cook, stirring occasionally, for about 10 minutes. Pour the mixture into a baking dish and sprinkle evenly with Parmesan cheese. Broil for about 5 minutes or until browned on top.

MAKES 4 TO 6 SERVINGS

SWISS VEGETABLE MEDLEY

1   16-ounce package frozen vegetable
    mix (broccoli, carrots, and
    cauliflower), thawed
1   10-ounce can condensed cream of
    mushroom soup
1   cup shredded Swiss cheese
⅓   cup sour cream
¼   teaspoon pepper
1   4-ounce jar diced pimientos, drained
1   3-ounce can French-fried onions

Preheat the oven to 350°. In a large mixing bowl combine the vegetables, soup, ½ cup Swiss cheese, sour cream, pepper, pimientos, and ½ can French-fried onions. Pour into a shallow 1-quart baking dish. Cover and bake for 30 minutes.

Sprinkle the remaining cheese and onions in diagonal rows across top. Bake, uncovered, for 5 more minutes or until the cheese is melted and the onions are golden brown.

MAKES 6 SERVINGS

MEXICAN RICE PILAF

2 tablespoons vegetable oil
2 medium onions, chopped
2 teaspoons minced garlic
3 cups vegetable stock
3 cups instant brown rice
1 tablespoon chili powder
1 jalapeño pepper, seeded and minced
1 teaspoon ground cumin
2 red bell peppers, chopped
2 large tomatoes, chopped
2 cups shredded Monterey Jack cheese

In a large saucepan heat the vegetable oil over medium-high heat. Add the onions and garlic, and cook for 3 minutes, stirring occasionally. Stir in the vegetable stock, rice, chili powder, jalapeño pepper, and cumin. Cover and bring to a boil. Reduce the heat, and simmer for 4 minutes, stirring occasionally. Stir in the bell peppers. Cover and simmer for 5 more minutes or until the liquid is absorbed. Fold in the tomatoes and Monterey Jack cheese.

MAKES 6 SERVINGS

VEGETABLE FETA RICE

1½ cups uncooked long grain rice

3   cups water

1   cup chopped red onion

1   cup chopped celery

1   cup chopped cucumber

1   cup feta cheese

1   tablespoon olive oil

2   tablespoons red wine vinegar

In a medium pot combine the rice and water. Bring to a boil. Cover, reduce the heat to low, and simmer the rice until tender. In a large mixing bowl combine the onion, celery, and cucumber. Crumble the feta cheese into the mixture. Pour the vegetable mixture over the cooked rice, cover, and let sit for 5 minutes. Toss the rice and vegetable mixture with oil and vinegar.

MAKES 4 TO 6 SERVINGS

CREAMY CALIFORNIA RICE

1 cup uncooked long grain rice

2 cups water

2 cups sour cream

2 4-ounce cans diced green chiles

2 cups Monterey Jack cheese, shredded

1 cup grated Parmesan cheese

Preheat the oven to 300°. Grease a shallow 1½-quart baking dish. In a medium pot combine the rice and water. Bring to a boil. Reduce the heat to low, cover, and simmer the rice until tender. Mix in the sour cream, chiles, and Monterey Jack cheese. Pour the rice mixture into the prepared baking dish, and sprinkle with Parmesan cheese. Bake for 30 minutes.

MAKES 6 SERVINGS

THREE-CHEESE RISOTTO

1   tablespoon olive oil
1   cup chopped onions
    Salt and pepper to taste
6   cups vegetable stock
2   teaspoons chopped garlic
16 ounces uncooked risotto (Arborio)
    rice
1   tablespoon butter or margarine
¼   cup whipping cream
¼   cup grated Parmesan cheese
¼   cup grated Romano cheese
¼   cup grated Asiago cheese
2   tablespoons chopped fresh chives

In a large saucepan heat the olive oil over medium heat. Add the onions, salt, and pepper, and sauté for 3 minutes, or until the onions are slightly soft. Add the vegetable stock and garlic. Bring to a boil, reduce the heat, and simmer for 6 minutes. Add the rice and simmer for 15 to 20 minutes, stirring frequently, until the rice is tender. Add the butter or margarine, cream, Parmesan cheese, Romano cheese, Asiago cheese, and chives, and simmer for 2 more minutes.

MAKES 8 TO 10 SERVINGS

ULTIMATE SCALLOPED POTATOES

1	cup whipping cream
⅓	cup milk
1	teaspoon salt
½	teaspoon pepper
2	cloves garlic, minced
6	medium potatoes, peeled and thinly sliced
1	cup shredded Swiss cheese
¼	cup shredded Parmesan cheese

Preheat the oven to 350°. Butter a shallow 1½-quart baking dish. In a medium saucepan combine the cream, milk, salt, pepper, and garlic. Cook just until bubbles begin to form around the sides of the pan. Remove from the heat and cool for 10 minutes.

Layer half of the potatoes in the prepared baking dish; top with half of the cream mixture and half of the Swiss and Parmesan cheeses. Repeat the layers. Bake for 1 hour or until the potatoes are tender.

MAKES 6 SERVINGS

CREAMY AU GRATIN POTATOES

4   russet potatoes, peeled and sliced thinly
1   medium onion, sliced
    Salt and pepper to taste
3   tablespoons butter or margarine
3   tablespoons all-purpose flour
½   teaspoon salt
2   cups milk
1½ cups shredded Cheddar cheese

Preheat the oven to 400°. Butter a 1-quart baking dish. Place half of the potatoes in the baking dish, and top with the onion slices. Add the remaining potatoes, and season with salt and pepper. In a medium saucepan melt the butter or margarine over medium heat. Gradually stir in the flour and salt, and mix thoroughly. Slowly add the milk, stirring constantly, until the mixture has thickened. Add the Cheddar cheese, stirring until melted. Pour the mixture over the potatoes, and cover the baking dish. Bake for 1 hour and 30 minutes.

MAKES 8 SERVINGS

CHEESY POTATO PANCAKES

3 cups shredded potatoes
2 cups shredded mild Cheddar cheese
1 10-ounce package frozen chopped broccoli, thawed
2 eggs
½ cup chopped onion
½ teaspoon thyme
  Salt and pepper to taste
¼ cup vegetable oil

In a large bowl mix together the potatoes, 1 cup Cheddar cheese, broccoli, eggs, onion, thyme, salt, and pepper. In a large skillet heat the vegetable oil over medium heat. For each pancake, fry 2 tablespoons of the potato mixture in vegetable oil until crisp and golden brown on both sides. Top the pancakes with the remaining cheese and broil 1 to 2 minutes or until the cheese melts.

MAKES 4 TO 6 SERVINGS

GARLIC POTATOES GRATIN

3   pounds red potatoes, peeled and thinly sliced
1½ cups shredded Gouda cheese
3   tablespoons butter or margarine
5   cloves garlic, minced
1½ cups whipping cream
1   teaspoon salt
½   teaspoon pepper

Preheat the oven to 325°. In a greased 9 x 13-inch baking dish layer half of the potatoes, followed by half of the Gouda cheese and the remaining potatoes. In a small skillet melt the butter or margarine over medium heat. Sauté the garlic until fragrant and golden brown, and pour over the potatoes. In a small bowl combine the cream, salt, and pepper, and pour evenly over the potatoes. Sprinkle with the remaining cheese. Bake for 1 hour and 15 minutes.

MAKES 8 SERVINGS

GOURMET CHEESE POTATOES

5	medium potatoes, peeled and chopped
¼	cup chopped onion
1	10-ounce can condensed Cheddar cheese soup
¾	cup milk
1½	cups sour cream
8	ounces American cheese, cubed
2	tablespoons butter or margarine, diced
½	cup shredded Cheddar cheese

Preheat the oven to 350°. In a large saucepan boil the potatoes in salted water until just tender, about 15 minutes. Drain and allow to cool. Place the potatoes and onion in a 9 x 13-inch baking dish. In a medium saucepan combine the soup, milk, sour cream, and American cheese. Heat, stirring, until the cheese is melted. Pour over the potatoes. Dot with butter or margarine and cover with Cheddar cheese. Bake for 1 hour.

MAKES 6 SERVINGS

CHEESY RANCH POTATOES

12 small new red potatoes, scrubbed
and halved
1 cup Ranch-style salad dressing
1 cup shredded Colby cheese
1 cup shredded Monterey Jack cheese
Pepper to taste

Preheat the oven to 350°. In a large saucepan boil the potatoes for 15 minutes or until just tender; drain. Place the potatoes on an ungreased baking sheet with the cut side up. Spread a spoonful of ranch dressing on top of each potato half. Sprinkle the potatoes with the Colby and Monterey Jack cheeses, and lightly dust with pepper. Bake for 5 minutes or until the cheese is melted.

MAKES 4 TO 6 SERVINGS

CREAMED NEW POTATOES

2½ pounds small red potatoes, peeled
  and chopped
8   ounces cream cheese, cubed
1   cup buttermilk
½   cup chopped green onion
1   teaspoon thyme
1   teaspoon tarragon
¼   teaspoon pepper
3   tablespoons finely chopped fresh
    parsley

Boil the potatoes in salted water for 15 to 20 minutes or until tender; drain and place in a large bowl. In a medium saucepan combine the cream cheese and buttermilk, stirring until the cheese is melted and the mixture is smooth. Remove from the heat, and add the green onion, thyme, tarragon, and pepper. Pour the mixture over the potatoes and mix well. Sprinkle with parsley.

MAKES 6 SERVINGS

COMPANY POTATOES

1   30-ounce package frozen hash brown potatoes, thawed

1   10-ounce can condensed cream of potato soup

1   10-ounce can condensed cream of celery soup

2   cups sour cream

¼   cup milk

½   cup chopped onion

1   teaspoon salt

½   teaspoon pepper

⅛   teaspoon dill weed

1½ cups shredded Cheddar cheese

Paprika to taste

Preheat the oven to 350°. Lightly oil a 9 x 13-inch baking dish. In a large bowl combine the hash browns, potato soup, celery soup, sour cream, milk, and onion, and mix well. Season with salt, pepper, and dill weed. Spoon into the prepared baking dish and sprinkle with Cheddar cheese and paprika. Bake for 1 hour and 15 minutes or until bubbly.

MAKES 8 SERVINGS

SWISS CHEESE POTATOES

1 30-ounce package frozen hash brown potatoes, thawed
½ cup butter or margarine, melted
2 cups whipping cream
3 cups grated Swiss cheese
Salt, pepper, and paprika to taste

Preheat the oven to 350°. Spread the potatoes in a 9 x 13-inch baking dish. Pour the butter or margarine over the potatoes, followed by the cream. Sprinkle the Swiss cheese, salt, pepper, and paprika over the top of the potatoes. Bake for 1 hour.

MAKES 6 TO 8 SERVINGS

CHIVE MASHED POTATOES

5 medium potatoes, peeled and cubed
4 ounces cream cheese, softened
2 tablespoons butter or margarine, softened
2 tablespoons snipped fresh chives
½ cup buttermilk
Salt and pepper to taste

In a large saucepan boil the potatoes in salted water for 25 to 30 minutes or until tender; drain. In a large mixing bowl beat the potatoes with an electric mixer until smooth. Add the cream cheese, butter or margarine, and chives, mixing well. Gradually beat in the buttermilk. Season with salt and pepper.

MAKES 4 TO 6 SERVINGS

GARLIC MASHED POTATOES

6	cloves garlic, peeled
¼	cup olive oil
7	large potatoes, peeled and cubed
½	cup milk
¼	cup grated Parmesan cheese
2	tablespoons butter or margarine, softened
	Salt and pepper to taste

Preheat the oven to 350°. Place the garlic cloves in a small baking dish. Drizzle with olive oil, cover, and bake for 45 minutes, or until golden brown. In a large saucepan boil the potatoes in salted water for 30 minutes or until tender. Drain and transfer to a large mixing bowl. Add the roasted garlic, milk, Parmesan cheese, and butter or margarine. Season with salt and pepper. Beat to the desired consistency with an electric mixer.

MAKES 8 SERVINGS

TWICE-BAKED POTATOES

4 large baking potatoes
¼ cup butter or margarine, softened
2 cups shredded Cheddar cheese
¾ cup sour cream
1 envelope Ranch-style salad dressing mix
1 tablespoon snipped fresh chives
1 clove garlic, minced
¼ cup chopped green onions

Bake potatoes at 400° for 1 hour and let cool. Reduce the oven temperature to 375°. Cut each potato in half lengthwise, and scoop out the pulp, leaving a thin shell. In a large mixing bowl combine the pulp with the butter or margarine; beat with an electric mixer until smooth. Stir in 1 cup of the Cheddar cheese, the sour cream, salad dressing mix, chives, and garlic. Spoon into the potato shells, and sprinkle with the remaining cheese. Place on a baking sheet, and bake at 375° for 15 to 20 minutes. Top with the green onions.

MAKES 8 SERVINGS

SEASONED POTATO WEDGES WITH SOUR CREAM DIP

⅓ cup all-purpose flour

⅓ cup grated Parmesan cheese

1 teaspoon paprika

⅓ cup milk

3 large baking potatoes, cut into wedges

¼ cup butter or margarine, melted

Sour Cream Dip:

2 cups sour cream

2 tablespoons shipped fresh chives

½ teaspoon garlic powder

Preheat the oven to 400°. Oil a large baking sheet. In a medium bowl combine the flour, Parmesan cheese, and paprika. Place the milk in a small bowl. Dip the potato wedges in milk, then dip in the flour mixture, coating well. Place on the prepared baking sheet. Drizzle the wedges with 2 tablespoons butter or margarine. Bake for 20 minutes. Turn the wedges, drizzle with the remaining butter or margarine, and bake 20 to 25 minutes longer or until the potatoes are tender and golden brown.

In a bowl combine the sour cream, chives, and garlic powder, and mix well. Serve with the warm potato wedges.

Makes 6 to 8 servings

DESSERTS

APPLE BUTTER COOKIES

1 cup sugar
1 cup butter or margarine, softened
¼ cup apple butter
1 egg
2½ cups all-purpose flour
1 cup finely shredded Cheddar cheese
½ teaspoon baking soda
½ teaspoon apple pie spice

In a large bowl mix together the sugar, butter or margarine, apple butter, and egg. Stir in the flour, Cheddar cheese, baking soda, and apple pie spice, and mix well. Cover and refrigerate for at least 2 hours.

Divide the cookie dough in half. Shape each half into a roll, about 1½ inches in diameter and 8 inches long. Wrap and refrigerate at least 4 hours.

Preheat the oven to 400°. Cut the rolls into thin slices. Place on an ungreased baking sheet, and bake for 8 minutes or until the edges are light brown.

MAKES 5 DOZEN

CHEESE AND CHOCOLATE CHIP COOKIES

8   ounces cream cheese, softened
1   cup butter or margarine, melted
¾   cup granulated sugar
¾   cup brown sugar, packed tightly
1   egg
1   teaspoon vanilla extract
2½ cups all-purpose flour
1   teaspoon baking powder
½   teaspoon salt
2   cups milk chocolate chips

Preheat the oven to 375°. Coat a large baking sheet with cooking spray. In a large bowl beat together the cream cheese, butter or margarine, granulated sugar, and brown sugar, until smooth. Blend in the egg and vanilla. Slowly add the flour, baking powder, and salt, and mix well. Stir in the chocolate chips. Drop rounded spoonfuls of batter onto the prepared baking sheet, and bake for 15 to 18 minutes or until the edges are slightly browned.

MAKES 2 DOZEN

CHOCOLATE SWIRLS

½ cup butter or margarine, softened
½ cup brown sugar, packed
½ cup granulated sugar
3 ounces cream cheese, softened
1 egg
1 teaspoon vanilla extract
2 cups all-purpose flour
½ teaspoon baking powder
¼ teaspoon salt
1 cup semisweet chocolate chips, melted

Preheat the oven to 350°. In a large bowl beat together the butter or margarine, brown sugar, and granulated sugar with an electric mixer until smooth. Beat in the cream cheese, egg, and vanilla. Gradually add the flour, baking powder, and salt to the cream cheese mixture, mixing well, to form a soft dough. Fold in the melted chocolate until the dough is just marbled. Drop the dough by heaping teaspoons onto an ungreased baking sheet, and bake for 10 to 12 minutes.

MAKES 4 DOZEN

COTTAGE CHEESE COOKIES

1 cup vegetable shortening

1¾ cups sugar

2 teaspoons vanilla extract

2 eggs

2¾ cups all-purpose flour

1 teaspoon baking powder

½ teaspoon baking soda

½ teaspoon salt

½ cup cocoa

1 cup cottage cheese

½ cup chopped pecans

⅓ cup powdered sugar

In a mixing bowl beat together the shortening, sugar, and vanilla until smooth. Beat in the eggs one at a time. Gradually add the flour, baking powder, baking soda, salt, and cocoa, mixing well. Fold in the cottage cheese and pecans. Cover and chill for 1 hour.

Preheat the oven to 350°. Place the powdered sugar in a small bowl. Roll the cookie dough into 1-inch balls, and roll each ball in the powdered sugar, coating well. Place 2 inches apart on a large baking sheet. Bake for 8 to 10 minutes.

MAKES 3 DOZEN

CREAM CHEESE COOKIES

½ cup butter or margarine

3 ounces cream cheese, softened

1 cup sugar

1 egg

4 1-ounce squares semisweet chocolate, melted

½ teaspoon vanilla extract

2 cups all-purpose flour

½ teaspoon baking powder

In a large bowl beat together the butter or margarine and cream cheese with an electric mixer. Add the sugar and beat until fluffy. Add the egg, melted chocolate, and vanilla, and beat well. Gradually add the flour and baking powder, beating until all the ingredients are mixed thoroughly. Cover and chill for at least 2 hours.

Preheat the oven to 375°. Coat a large baking sheet with cooking spray. Using a lightly floured rolling pin, roll the cookie dough out flat on a lightly floured surface. Cut into circles or other shapes with cookie cutters, and place on the prepared baking sheet. Bake for 8 to 10 minutes.

MAKES 5 DOZEN

CHEDDAR FRUIT DROPS

½ cup butter or margarine, melted

¼ cup sugar

¼ cup brown sugar, firmly packed

1 egg

1 tablespoon vanilla extract

1½ cups all-purpose flour

½ teaspoon baking soda

½ teaspoon salt

1½ cups grated sharp Cheddar cheese

8 ounces pineapple, crushed and drained

¼ cup chopped maraschino cherries

Preheat the oven to 375°. In a mixing bowl combine the butter or margarine and sugars until light and fluffy. Stir in the egg and vanilla. Add the flour, baking soda, and salt, and blend well. Stir in the cheese, pineapple, and cherries. Drop the dough by rounded teaspoonfuls onto an ungreased cookie sheet, and bake for 15 minutes.

MAKES 2 DOZEN

RICOTTA COOKIES

1	cup butter or margarine, softened
2	cups sugar
2	eggs
2	cups ricotta cheese
2	teaspoons vanilla extract
4	cups all-purpose flour
1	teaspoon baking powder
1	teaspoon baking soda

Frosting:

½	cup milk
½	teaspoon butter or margarine
½	teaspoon shortening
4	cups powdered sugar
1	tablespoon lemon extract
½	cup colored candy sprinkles

Preheat the oven to 350°. Grease a large baking sheet. In a large bowl beat together 1 cup butter or margarine and 2 cups sugar with an electric mixer. Beat in the eggs, one at a time, until fluffy. Stir in the ricotta cheese and vanilla. Gradually add the flour, baking powder, and baking soda, mixing well. Drop by rounded spoonfuls onto the prepared baking sheet. Bake for 8 to 10 minutes.

In a small saucepan warm the milk, ½ teaspoon butter or margarine, and the shortening. Cook over medium heat, stirring occasionally, until melted. Transfer to a bowl and gradually stir in the powdered sugar and lemon extract. Dip each cookie halfway into the frosting and sprinkle with candy sprinkles. Let cool before serving.

MAKES 4 DOZEN

CRANBERRY CHEESE BARS

Crust:

2   cups all-purpose flour

1½ cups rolled oats

¾   cup brown sugar

1   cup butter or margarine, softened

Filling:

8   ounces cream cheese, softened

1   14-ounce can sweetened condensed milk

¼   cup lemon juice

1   tablespoon brown sugar

2   tablespoons cornstarch

1   16-ounce can cranberry sauce

Preheat the oven to 350°. In a medium bowl stir together the flour, oats, and ¾ cup brown sugar. Cut in the butter or margarine, until the mixture is crumbly. Reserve 1½ cups of the mixture. Press the remaining mixture into the bottom of a 9 x 13-inch baking dish and bake for 15 minutes.

In a small bowl beat together the cream cheese and condensed milk until light and fluffy. Stir in the lemon juice and spread the mixture evenly over the prepared crust. In a bowl combine the brown sugar, cornstarch, and cranberry sauce. Spoon over the cream cheese layer. Sprinkle with the reserved crust mixture. Bake for 35 to 40 minutes, or until the top is golden. Let cool completely, and cut into bars to serve.

MAKES 2 DOZEN

CREAM CHEESE BROWNIES

4   1-ounce squares unsweetened
    chocolate

¾   cup butter or margarine

2⅓ cups sugar

4   eggs

1   teaspoon vanilla extract

1⅛ cups all-purpose flour

1½ cups chopped walnuts

8   ounces cream cheese

Preheat the oven to 350°. Coat the bottom and sides of a
9 x 13-inch baking dish with cooking spray. In a small pan mix the
chocolate and butter or margarine over low heat, stirring constantly, until the chocolate is melted and the mixture is smooth.
Transfer the chocolate mixture to a medium bowl, and stir in 2
cups sugar, 3 eggs, and the vanilla. Add 1 cup flour and walnuts,
and stir until the mixture is well blended. Pour the chocolate mixture into the prepared baking dish. In a small bowl beat together
the cream cheese, ⅓ cup sugar, 1 egg, and ⅛ cup flour until well
blended. Spoon the mixture evenly over the chocolate layer. Bake
for 30 to 35 minutes. Cool and cut into squares.

MAKES 2 DOZEN

GLAZED RASPBERRY BARS

1   cup butter or margarine, softened
¼   cup sugar
½   cup milk
1   teaspoon vanilla extract
2   eggs
3   cups all-purpose flour
3   teaspoons baking powder
1   teaspoon salt
1   20-ounce can raspberry pie filling

Glaze:
1   tablespoon butter or margarine, softened
1   tablespoon shortening
1   ounce cream cheese, softened
2   tablespoons marshmallow creme
⅔   cup powdered sugar
1   tablespoon milk

In a mixing bowl beat together 1 cup butter or margarine, sugar, milk, and vanilla with an electric mixer. Beat in the eggs one at a time. Gradually add the flour, baking powder, and salt, mixing well. Chill for 2 hours or until firm.

Preheat the oven to 350°. Grease a 10 x 15-inch baking sheet. With a lightly floured rolling pin, roll out half of the dough onto a flat floured surface, to form a large (about 9 x 14 inches) rectangle. Carefully transfer the crust to the prepared baking sheet.

Spread the raspberry pie filling evenly over the top of the crust. Roll out the remaining dough to ¼-inch thickness. Cut into ½-inch-wide strips. Arrange half of the strips lengthwise about ½ inch apart over the top of the pie filling. Arrange the remaining strips crosswise. Bake for 30 minutes or until golden brown. Cool on a wire rack.

In a medium bowl beat together 1 tablespoon butter or margarine, the shortening, cream cheese, and marshmallow creme until smooth. Add the powdered sugar and milk and mix well. Drizzle the glaze over bars. Chill for at least 2 hours; cut into bars before serving.

MAKES 2 DOZEN

MINT CHOCOLATE SQUARES

3 eggs

1½ cups sugar

2 teaspoons vanilla extract

10 tablespoons butter or margarine

3 1-ounce squares unsweetened chocolate, chopped

1 cup all-purpose flour

8 ounces cream cheese, softened

1 tablespoon cornstarch

1 14-ounce can sweetened condensed milk

1 teaspoon peppermint extract

Green food coloring

1 cup semisweet chocolate chips

½ cup whipping cream

Preheat the oven to 350°. Grease a 9 x 13-inch baking dish. In a mixing bowl beat together 2 eggs, the sugar, and vanilla with an electric mixer. In a saucepan over low heat combine 8 tablespoons butter or margarine and the unsweetened chocolate squares, stirring until melted. Stir into the egg mixture, and beat until well blended. Gradually beat in the flour. Spread into the prepared baking dish. Bake for 15 to 20 minutes or until the top is set. Remove from the oven and let cool.

In a mixing bowl beat the cream cheese and remaining butter. Add the cornstarch and beat until smooth. Gradually beat in the milk and remaining egg. Add the peppermint extract and 3 to 4 drops green food coloring, stirring until the color is thoroughly blended. Pour into the baking dish over the chocolate layer. Bake for 15 to 20 minutes or until the center is almost set. Allow to cool.

In a saucepan over low heat combine the chocolate chips and cream, stirring, until the chocolate chips are melted and the mixture is thoroughly blended. Pour over the cream cheese layer. Chill for 2 hours or until ready to serve; cut into small squares.

MAKES 4 DOZEN

PERFECT PUMPKIN BARS

4   eggs
1⅔ cups sugar
1   cup vegetable oil
1   15-ounce can pumpkin purée
2   cups all-purpose flour
2   teaspoons baking powder
1   teaspoon baking soda
2   teaspoons cinnamon
1   teaspoon salt

Frosting:
3   ounces cream cheese, softened
½   cup butter or margarine, softened
1   teaspoon vanilla extract
2   cups powdered sugar

Preheat the oven to 350°. In a large mixing bowl combine the eggs, sugar, oil, and pumpkin purée. Beat with an electric mixer until light and fluffy. Sift the flour, baking powder, baking soda, cinnamon, and salt into a bowl. Gradually stir into the pumpkin mixture until thoroughly combined. Spread the batter evenly into a 10 x 15-inch baking pan. Bake for 25 to 30 minutes, and let cool.

In a medium bowl beat together the cream cheese and butter or margarine. Stir in the vanilla. Slowly add the powdered sugar, beating with an electric mixer, until the mixture is smooth. Spread evenly on top of the bars. Cut into squares to serve.

MAKES 2 DOZEN

CHOCOLATE CREAM CHEESE CUPCAKES

1½ cups all-purpose flour
1   cup sugar
¼   cup cocoa
1   teaspoon baking soda
½   teaspoon salt
1   cup water
⅓   cup vegetable oil
1   tablespoon cider vinegar
1   teaspoon vanilla extract

Topping:
8   ounces cream cheese, softened
1   egg
⅓   cup sugar
⅛   teaspoon salt
1   cup semisweet chocolate chips

Preheat the oven to 350°. Line 2 12-cup muffin pans with paper liners. In a large bowl mix together the flour, 1 cup sugar, cocoa, baking soda, and ½ teaspoon salt. Gradually add the water, oil, vinegar, and vanilla, stirring until well blended. Spoon the mixture evenly into muffin cups, filling the cups two-thirds full.

In a medium bowl beat together the cream cheese, egg, ⅓ cup sugar, and ⅛ teaspoon salt until light and fluffy. Stir in the chocolate chips. Spoon about 1 tablespoon of the cream cheese mixture into each muffin tin. Bake for 25 to 30 minutes.

MAKES 24 SERVINGS

MINI ALMOND CAKES

12 vanilla wafers

11 ounces cream cheese, softened

¼ cup sugar

½ teaspoon almond extract

2 eggs

¼ cup chopped almonds, toasted

Preheat the oven to 350°. Line a 12-cup muffin pan with paper liners. Place 1 vanilla wafer, flat side down, in each cup. In a bowl beat together the cream cheese, sugar, and almond extract until fluffy. Beat in the eggs, one at a time. Spoon the mixture into the muffin cups, filling the cups three-fourths full. Sprinkle with almonds. Bake for 20 minutes and let cool. Cover and chill for 2 hours or until ready to serve.

MAKES 12 SERVINGS

RASPBERRY CUPCAKES

¾ cup graham cracker crumbs

¼ cup chopped pecans

3 tablespoons butter or margarine, melted

1 cup fresh raspberries

4 ounces cream cheese, softened

1 12-ounce can sweetened condensed milk

1 cup frozen whipped topping, thawed

Line a 12-cup muffin pan with paper liners. In a medium bowl combine the graham cracker crumbs, crushed pecans, and melted butter or margarine, mixing well to blend. Spoon the mixture evenly into the baking cups, pressing with a spoon to firm. In a blender purée the raspberries until smooth and set aside. In a medium bowl beat the cream cheese with an electric mixer until fluffy. Add the condensed milk and half of the raspberry purée and mix until well blended. Fold in the whipped topping. Spoon the mixture evenly into the baking cups. Freeze for at least 4 hours. Drizzle the remaining raspberry purée over the cups before serving.

MAKES 12 SERVINGS

HAWAIIAN SHEET CAKE

3   cups all-purpose flour
2   cups sugar
1   teaspoon baking powder
1   teaspoon salt
1   teaspoon cinnamon
3   eggs, beaten
1½ cups vegetable oil
2   cups diced bananas
2   teaspoons vanilla extract
1   8-ounce can crushed pineapple, drained
1   cup chopped pecans

Frosting:
½   cup chopped pecans
8   ounces cream cheese, softened
½   cup butter or margarine, softened
4   cups powdered sugar
1   teaspoon vanilla extract

Preheat the oven to 350°. Grease and flour an 11 x 17-inch baking pan. In a large bowl combine the flour, sugar, baking powder, salt, and cinnamon. Add the eggs and oil, and stir until moistened. Stir in the bananas, 2 teaspoons vanilla, the pineapple, and 1 cup pecans. Spread evenly onto the prepared baking pan. Bake for 25 to 30 minutes and let cool.

In a medium bowl beat together ½ cup pecans, the cream cheese, butter or margarine, powdered sugar, and 1 teaspoon vanilla until light and fluffy. Spread the frosting over the cooled cake.

MAKES 24 SERVINGS

PINEAPPLE CARROT CAKE

1¾ cups sugar

1½ cups vegetable oil

4 eggs

2 teaspoons vanilla extract

2½ cups all-purpose flour

2 teaspoons baking soda

2 teaspoons cinnamon

1 teaspoon salt

2 cups shredded carrots

1 8-ounce can crushed pineapple,
   undrained

1 cup chopped walnuts

Frosting:

16 ounces cream cheese, softened

½ cup butter or margarine, softened

1 teaspoon vanilla extract

3 cups powdered sugar

Preheat the oven to 350°. Coat a 9 x 13-inch baking dish with cooking spray. In a large bowl beat together the sugar, oil, eggs, and vanilla with an electric mixer until well blended. Gradually beat in the flour, baking soda, cinnamon, and salt, until the mixture is smooth. Stir in the carrots, pineapple with juice, and nuts. Spread the batter evenly in the prepared baking dish, and bake for 45 to 50 minutes. Remove from the oven and let cool.

In a medium bowl beat together the cream cheese, butter or margarine, and vanilla with an electric mixer until light and creamy, about 2 minutes. Gradually beat in the powdered sugar, beating until fluffy. Generously spread the frosting over the cake.

MAKES 16 SERVINGS

CHERRY CHEESE COFFEE CAKE

2   8-ounce packages refrigerated
    crescent rolls
8   ounces cream cheese, softened
¼   cup powdered sugar
1   egg
½   teaspoon vanilla extract
1   20-ounce can cherry pie filling
    All-purpose flour

Glaze:
½   cup powdered sugar
2½ teaspoons milk

Preheat the oven to 350°. Unroll the crescent dough and separate into 16 triangles, reserving 4 triangles. Arrange 12 triangles in a circle on a 15-inch round pizza pan. With a lightly floured rolling pin, roll the dough into a 14-inch circle. In a medium bowl beat together the cream cheese, powdered sugar, egg, and vanilla, until smooth. Spread the cream cheese mixture over the dough, and top with the cherry pie filling. Cut the reserved dough into thirds lengthwise, and arrange on top of the pie in a spoke-like fashion. Bake for 25 to 30 minutes or until golden brown.

In a small bowl, whisk together the powdered sugar and milk until smooth. Drizzle the glaze over the coffee cake before serving.

MAKES 12 SERVINGS

DECADENT TURTLE CHEESECAKE

Crust:

2   cups vanilla wafer crumbs
6   tablespoons butter or margarine, melted

Filling:

14 ounces individually wrapped caramels
1   5-ounce can condensed milk
1   cup chopped pecans, toasted
24 ounces cream cheese
½   cup sugar
1½ teaspoons vanilla extract
2   eggs
½   cup semisweet chocolate chips, melted

Preheat the oven to 350°. Butter a 9-inch pie pan. In a medium bowl mix together the vanilla wafer crumbs and melted butter or margarine. Press the mixture into the bottom and sides of the prepared pie pan. Place the pan on a baking sheet and bake for 10 minutes. Remove from the oven and let cool.

In a double boiler melt the caramels in the condensed milk, stirring constantly until smooth. Pour the caramel mixture into the pie crust. Sprinkle the pecans over top. In a bowl beat the cream cheese, sugar, and vanilla with an electric mixer until smooth. Add the eggs, one at a time, beating until smooth. Gently stir the melted chocolate chips into the cheese mixture. Pour the mixture into the pie crust. Bake at 350° for 40 minutes or until just set. Chill for several hours before serving.

MAKES 8 SERVINGS

CHOCOLATE CHEESECAKE

Crust:

1¼ cups graham cracker crumbs

½ cup sugar

¼ cup cocoa

6 tablespoons butter or margarine, melted

Filling:

24 ounces cream cheese, softened

¾ cup sugar

3 eggs

1 cup semisweet chocolate chips, melted

1 teaspoon almond extract

½ teaspoon vanilla extract

Topping:

¼ cup semisweet chocolate chips

⅓ cup whipping cream

1 tablespoon honey

Preheat the oven to 350°. Grease a 9-inch pie pan. In a bowl combine the graham cracker crumbs, sugar, and cocoa. Stir in the butter or margarine. Press into the bottom and sides of the prepared pie pan and set aside.

In a small mixing bowl beat the cream cheese and sugar until smooth. Add the eggs, and beat on low speed until just combined.

Stir in the melted chocolate, almond extract, and vanilla extract until just blended. Pour into the crust. Bake for 45 to 50 minutes or until the center is almost set. Cool, cover, and refrigerate for at least 1 hour.

In a saucepan over low heat melt ¼ cup chocolate chips, cream, and honey, stirring constantly until smooth and well blended. Remove from the heat and cool for 5 minutes. Pour the topping over the cheesecake. Chill for at least 4 hours or until ready to serve.

MAKES 8 SERVINGS

NECTARINE CHEESECAKE

Crust:
2   cups graham cracker crumbs
2   teaspoons sugar
½   teaspoon cinnamon
6   tablespoons butter or margarine, melted

Filling:
12 ounces cream cheese, softened
⅓   cup sugar
½   teaspoon vanilla extract
2   eggs
2   nectarines, peeled, pitted and diced

In a medium bowl mix together the graham cracker crumbs, sugar, cinnamon, and butter or margarine until well blended. Press into the bottom and sides of a 9-inch pie pan. Refrigerate.

Preheat the oven to 350°. In a medium bowl beat together the cream cheese, sugar, and vanilla until smooth. Beat in the eggs, one at a time, until well blended. Fold in half of the nectarine pieces, and pour the mixture into the pie crust. Bake for 30 to 35 minutes. Let cool to room temperature, then chill for at least 2 hours or until firm. Sprinkle the remaining nectarine pieces over top before serving.

MAKES 8 SERVINGS

DELICIOUS NUTRITIOUS CHEESECAKE

Crust:

¾ cup whole wheat dry breadcrumbs

¼ cup wheat germ

2 tablespoons sugar

2 tablespoons sesame seeds

5 tablespoons butter or margarine, melted

Filling:

8 ounces cream cheese, softened

3 tablespoons honey

1 cup plain yogurt

1 teaspoon vanilla extract

1 teaspoon grated orange peel

⅓ cup sliced almonds

Preheat the oven to 375°. In a medium bowl mix together the breadcrumbs, wheat germ, sugar, sesame seeds, and butter or margarine. Press the mixture firmly into the bottom and sides of a 9-inch pie pan. Bake for 8 minutes. Remove from the oven and let cool.

In a large bowl beat the cream cheese with honey until fluffy. Gradually stir in the yogurt until smooth. Add the vanilla and orange peel, and mix well. Spread the mixture into the pie crust. Sprinkle the almonds evenly over the filling. Cover and refrigerate for several hours before serving.

MAKES 8 SERVINGS

RICOTTA CHEESECAKE

Crust:
2   cups graham cracker crumbs
½   cup powdered sugar
½   cup butter or margarine, melted

Filling:
1   tablespoon plain gelatin mix
½   cup cold water
1   3-ounce package lemon gelatin mix
1¾ cups hot water
½   cup sugar
¼   cup lemon juice
2   cups whipping cream, whipped
2   cups ricotta cheese, whipped
    Strawberries, sliced

In a medium bowl mix together the graham cracker crumbs, powdered sugar, and butter or margarine. Press the mixture into the bottom and sides of a 9 x 13-inch baking dish, reserving about ½ cup of the mixture for garnish.

Dissolve the plain gelatin in ½ cup cold water. In a large bowl combine the lemon gelatin, 1¾ cups hot water, sugar, lemon juice, and plain gelatin mixture, and mix well. Chill for 30 minutes or until syrupy.

Beat the gelatin mixture with an electric mixer. Fold the whipped cream into the gelatin mixture. Add the ricotta cheese, and mix well. Pour into the graham cracker crust. Sprinkle the reserved graham cracker mixture over top, and chill for several hours. Top with strawberry slices before serving.

MAKES 8 SERVINGS

TRIPLE CHOCOLATE PIE

Crust:

1¼ cups graham cracker crumbs

½ cup sugar

¼ cup cocoa

6   tablespoons butter or margarine,
    melted

Filling:

1   cup semisweet chocolate chips,
    melted

8   ounces cream cheese, softened

1   4-ounce package chocolate instant
    pudding mix

1½ cups milk

    Whipped topping

Grease a 9-inch pie pan. In a large bowl combine the graham cracker crumbs, sugar, and cocoa, and stir in the butter or margarine. Press the mixture into the bottom and sides of the prepared pie pan and set aside.

In a large bowl beat together the melted chocolate and cream cheese with an electric mixer until smooth. Add the chocolate pudding mix and milk. Beat at low speed until the mixture is smooth and creamy. Pour the mixture into the crust and chill for several hours. Serve with whipped topping.

MAKES 8 SERVINGS

EASY PEANUT BUTTER PIE

8   ounces cream cheese, softened
1   cup sugar
1   teaspoon vanilla extract
⅔ cup peanut butter
8   ounces frozen whipped topping, thawed
1   9-inch pie crust, baked

In a medium bowl beat together the cream cheese, sugar, and vanilla. Add the peanut butter and mix well. Fold in the whipped topping until completely blended. Spoon the peanut butter mixture into the pie crust. Freeze for 2 hours or until ready to serve.

MAKES 8 SERVINGS

GERMAN CHOCOLATE PIE

Crust:

1¾ cups finely chopped walnuts

3 tablespoons butter or margarine, melted

Filling:

4 ounces cream cheese, softened

2 tablespoons sugar

4 1-ounce squares sweet chocolate, melted

⅓ cup milk

8 ounces frozen whipped topping

In a medium bowl combine the walnuts and butter or margarine, and mix well. Press the walnut mixture into the bottom and sides of a 9-inch pie pan, and chill.

In a mixing bowl beat together the cream cheese and sugar. Add the melted chocolate and milk, beating until well blended. Refrigerate the mixture for about 10 minutes to cool. Fold in the whipped topping, and spoon the mixture into the pie crust. Freeze for 4 hours or until ready to serve.

MAKES 8 SERVINGS

KEY LIME CHEESE PIE

Crust:
¼ cup butter or margarine, melted
1¼ cups graham cracker crumbs
¼ cup sugar
¼ cup finely chopped pecans

Filling:
16 ounces cream cheese, softened
4 ounces key lime juice
4 egg yolks, beaten
1 14-ounce can sweetened condensed milk
¼ cup graham cracker crumbs

Preheat the oven to 350°. In a medium bowl combine the butter or margarine, 1¼ cups graham cracker crumbs, sugar, and pecans. Press into the bottom and sides of a 9-inch pie pan, and bake for 10 minutes.

In a mixing bowl beat together the cream cheese, key lime juice, and egg yolks. Gradually add the condensed milk, until well blended. Pour into the pie crust, and chill for several hours. Sprinkle with ¼ cup graham cracker crumbs before serving.

MAKES 8 SERVINGS

PEACHES AND CREAM CHEESE PIE

12 ounces cream cheese, softened
¼ cup sugar
½ teaspoon vanilla extract
2 eggs
1 9-inch pie crust, baked
4 peaches, peeled and thinly sliced
2 tablespoons apple jelly
2 tablespoons crumbled blue cheese

Preheat the oven to 350°. In a medium bowl combine the cream cheese, sugar, and vanilla. Beat with an electric mixer until smooth. Beat in the eggs, one at a time, until fluffy. Pour the mixture into the pie crust. Arrange the peaches evenly on top of the filling. In a small saucepan melt half of the jelly over low heat. Brush the tops of the peaches with jelly. Bake for 30 to 35 minutes or until the center is almost set. Heat the remaining jelly, and brush over the top of the pie. Let the pie cool, then cover and chill for several hours. Sprinkle with blue cheese just before serving.

MAKES 8 SERVINGS

RICOTTA TORTE

1	tablespoon butter or margarine, melted
¼	cup graham cracker crumbs
2	cups ricotta cheese
5	egg yolks
½	cup sugar
½	teaspoon salt
1	teaspoon grated lemon rind
1	tablespoon lemon juice

Preheat the oven to 325°. In a bowl combine the butter or margarine and graham cracker crumbs. Lightly sprinkle the mixture into the bottom of a 9-inch pie pan. In a large bowl beat together the ricotta cheese, egg yolks, sugar, salt, lemon rind, and lemon juice with an electric mixer. Pour the cheese mixture over the graham cracker crumbs. Bake for about 35 minutes or until golden. Cool before serving.

MAKES 8 SERVINGS

STRAWBERRY CHOCOLATE TART

Crust:

14 chocolate cream-filled sandwich
cookies, crumbled

¾ cup finely chopped pecans

2 tablespoons butter or margarine, melted

Filling:

½ teaspoon unflavored gelatin mix

⅔ cup whipping cream

3 ounces cream cheese, softened

8 ounces white baking chocolate,
coarsely chopped

2 cups fresh strawberries, tops cut off
and halved

In a large bowl mix together the cookies and pecans. Add the butter or margarine, and mix thoroughly. Press the mixture into the bottom and sides of a 9-inch pie pan. Refrigerate.

In a small bowl sprinkle the gelatin over the cream. Let stand until the gelatin is softened, about 5 minutes. In a medium bowl beat the cream cheese with an electric mixer until smooth. Add the cream mixture and beat until just smooth. Transfer the mixture to a small saucepan. Add the white baking chocolate and cook at medium heat, stirring constantly, until the gelatin is dissolved and the chocolate is melted. Pour the mixture into the pie crust. Refrigerate at least 1 hour and 30 minutes, or until firm.

Arrange the strawberries in the center of the tart before serving.

MAKES 8 SERVINGS

ULTIMATE STRAWBERRY PIE

Crust:

1½ cups all-purpose flour

½ teaspoon salt

2   tablespoons sugar

½ cup vegetable oil

2   tablespoons milk

Filling:

11 ounces cream cheese, softened

4   tablespoons sugar

4   cups fresh strawberries, tops cut off
    and halved

2   1-ounce squares semisweet
    chocolate, melted

Preheat the oven to 400°. In a medium bowl combine the flour, salt, sugar, vegetable oil, and milk. Mix well and press into the sides and bottom of a 9-inch pie pan. Bake for 12 to 15 minutes or until golden brown. Allow to cool.

In a mixing bowl beat the cream cheese and sugar until smooth. Add 1 cup of strawberries and beat well. Spread into the cooled pie crust. Dip the tips of the remaining strawberries in melted chocolate, and arrange on top of the pie. Chill for several hours before serving.

MAKES 8 SERVINGS

BANANA PUDDING

8	ounces cream cheese
1	14-ounce can sweetened condensed milk
1	5-ounce package instant vanilla pudding mix
3	cups milk
1	teaspoon vanilla extract
8	ounces frozen whipped topping, thawed
3	cups coarsely crushed vanilla wafers
4	bananas, sliced

In a large bowl beat the cream cheese with an electric mixer until fluffy. Beat in the condensed milk, pudding mix, milk, and vanilla until smooth. Fold in half of the whipped topping.

Line the bottom of a 9 x 13-inch baking dish with crushed vanilla wafers. Arrange the sliced bananas evenly over the wafers. Spread with the pudding mixture. Top with the remaining whipped topping. Chill until ready to serve.

MAKES 12 SERVINGS

CHERRY CHEESE TRIANGLES

⅓ cup finely chopped dried cherries
1 cup boiling water
1 egg, beaten
1 cup ricotta cheese
½ cup powdered sugar
¼ cup chopped pecans, toasted
12 sheets frozen phyllo dough, thawed
Vegetable oil

Preheat the oven to 375°. Place the cherries in a medium bowl. Pour boiling water over the cherries and let stand for 10 minutes. Drain. In a medium bowl beat the egg, ricotta cheese, and powdered sugar until smooth. Stir in the cherries and pecans.

Unfold the phyllo dough. Cut the sheets lengthwise in half. Place a half sheet of phyllo on a wax paper–lined surface. Brush the phyllo sheet lightly with vegetable oil and fold the sheet in half lengthwise, to form a long strip. Lightly brush the top of the phyllo sheet with oil. Spoon a tablespoon of cherry mixture about 1 inch from one end of the phyllo sheet. Fold the end over the filling at a 45-degree angle to form a triangle. Continue folding to the opposite end of the phyllo dough. Place the triangle on an ungreased baking sheet, and repeat with the remaining phyllo dough and cherry mixture.

Brush the tops of the triangles with oil. Bake for about 15 minutes or until golden.

MAKES 2 DOZEN

CHERRY MACAROON DELIGHT

2   cups coarsely crushed macaroon
    cookies
1   15-ounce can pitted cherries, drained
1   cup whipping cream
3   ounces cream cheese, softened

Sprinkle 1¼ cups of the cookie crumbs into an 8-inch square baking pan, reserving the remaining crumbs. Place the cherries in a blender and process until coarsely chopped. In a medium bowl beat together the whipping cream and cream cheese until stiff. Fold in the cherries. Spread evenly in the pan, and top with the reserved cookie crumbs. Cover and freeze for at least 4 hours, or until ready to serve.

MAKES 9 SERVINGS

COCONUT CANDY

¼ cup butter or margarine, softened
4 ounces cream cheese, softened
1 teaspoon vanilla extract
4 cups powdered sugar
2½ cups flaked coconut
2 tablespoons cinnamon

In a medium bowl beat the butter or margarine and cream cheese together with an electric mixer until fluffy. Add the vanilla and powdered sugar and beat until smooth. Stir in the coconut. Place the cinnamon in a small bowl. Form the candy mixture into balls and roll in the cinnamon to coat. Place on a large baking sheet and chill for several hours before serving.

MAKES 5 DOZEN

CREAM CHEESE FUDGE

6 ounces cream cheese, softened
¼ cup butter or margarine, softened
1 teaspoon vanilla extract
¼ teaspoon salt
⅔ cup cocoa
4 cups powdered sugar
1 cup coarsely chopped pecans

In a large bowl beat together the cream cheese, butter or margarine, vanilla, and salt with an electric mixer until smooth. Gradually beat in the cocoa and powdered sugar. Stir in the pecans and mix well. Press the mixture into an 8-inch square pan. Refrigerate for about 3 hours or until firm. Cut into 1½-inch squares.

MAKES 2 DOZEN

WEIGHTS AND MEASURES

Equivalents

Food	Amount	Equals About
Hard and Semisoft Cheeses (Cheddar, Monterey Jack, etc.)	4 ounces	1 cup
Soft Cheeses (Cream Cheese, Cottage Cheese)	8 ounces	1 cup
Apple	1 medium	1 cup chopped
Banana	1 medium	1 sliced
Carrot	1 medium	⅔ cup shredded
Celery	1 stalk	½ cup sliced
Bell Pepper	1 medium	1 cup chopped
Onion	1 medium	½ cup chopped
Tomato	1 medium	1 cup chopped
Zucchini	2 medium	2 cups sliced

Substitutions

Food	Amount	Substitution
Beer	1 cup	1 cup vegetable stock
Brown Sugar	1 cup	1 cup white sugar and 2 cups powdered sugar
Cornstarch	1 tablespoon	2 tablespoons flour
Chocolate, unsweetened	1 ounce	3 tablespoons cocoa and 1 tablespoon shortening
Chocolate, semisweet	1 ounce	1 ounce unsweetened chocolate and 1 tablespoon sugar
Lemon Juice	1 teaspoon	1 teaspoon vinegar
Wine	1 cup	1 cup apple cider or 1 cup apple juice

Measurements

Amount	Equals
3 teaspoons	1 tablespoon
16 tablespoons	1 cup
2 cups	1 pint
4 cups	1 quart

INDEX

ABOUT THE AUTHOR

Tonya Buell lives in Chandler, Arizona, with her family and loves to experiment with new recipes. This is her fourth book.

Printed in the USA
CPSIA information can be obtained
at www.ICGtesting.com
JSHW082227140824
68134JS00016B/776